# Soundings

D1564305

*Issue 12*

# Transversal politics

EDITORS
Stuart Hall
Doreen Massey
Michael Rustin

GUEST EDITORS
Cynthia Cockburn
Lynette Hunter

POETRY EDITOR
Carole Satyamurti

REVIEWS EDITORS
Becky Hall and
Susanna Rustin

ART EDITOR
Tim Davison

EDITORIAL OFFICE
Lawrence & Wishart
99a Wallis Road
London E9 5LN

MARKETING CONSULTANT
Mark Perryman

ADVERTISEMENTS
Write for information to Soundings,
c/o Lawrence & Wishart

SUBSCRIPTIONS
1999 subscription rates are (for three issues):
**UK:** Institutions £70, Individuals £35
**Rest of the world:** Institutions £80, Individuals £45

ISSN 1362 6620
ISBN  0 85315 902 5

Text setting Art Services, Norwich
Cover photograph:  © Jane Plastow

Printed in Great Britain by
Cambridge University Press, Cambridge

Soundings is published three
times a year, in autumn,
spring and summer by:
**Soundings Ltd**
**c/o  Lawrence & Wishart**
**99a Wallis Road**
**London E9 5LN**

# CONTENTS

**Notes on contributors**                                              *v*

**Editorial: Space for Co-existence?**                                  7
Doreen Massey

***Ein Ding ist ein Thing* – A Philosophical Platform for a Left**     12
**(European) Party**
Bruno Latour

**The Sharp Edge of Stephen's City**                                   26
Nick Jeffrey

**Poems**                                                              44
Gregory Warren Wilson, Michael Young, Elizabeth Barrett,
Felicity Wyvern, Okello Oculi

**The Changing Debate in Scotland: Devolution, Home Rule and**         49
**Self-Government**
Gerry Hassan

**Reviews**                                                            66
Jo Littler, Mike Waite, Jude Rosen

────────────────── **Part 2 Transversal Politics** ──────────────────

**Introduction: Transversal Politics and Translating Practices**       88
Cynthia Cockburn and Lynette Hunter

**What is 'Transversal Politics?**
Nira Yuval-Davis

**Crossing Borders: Comparing Ways of Handling Conflictual**           94
**Differences**
Cynthia Cockburn

──────────────── Continued on next page ────────────────

*Continued from previous page*

**Difficult Alliances: Treading the Minefield of Identity and Solidarity Politics**    *115*
Pragna Patel

**Inclusive Movements/Movements for Inclusion**    *127*
Marie Mulholland and Pragna Patel

**The Values of Community Writing**    *144*
Lynette Hunter and Rebecca O'Rourke

**Theatre and Reconciliation: Reflections on work in Northern Ireland and Eritrea**    *153*
Gerri Moriarty and Jane Plastow

**Sharing Stories**    *163*
MAMA East African Women's Group

**The Way I Live**    *175*
Rosie

# NOTES ON CONTRIBUTORS

**Elizabeth Barrett**'s first poetry collection, *Walking on Tiptoe*, was published by Staple First Editions in 1998.

**Cynthia Cockburn** is a Research Professor in the Department of Sociology at City University, London, and co-ordinator of the action-research project Women Building Bridges, reported in her book *The Space Between Us: Negotiating Gender and National Identities in Conflict*, Zed Books 1998.

**Gerry Hassan** is Director of the Centre for Scottish Public Policy - an independent Scottish centre-left think tank. He is editor of, and a contributor to, the recently published collection *A Guide to the Scottish Parliament: The Shape of Things To Come*.

**Lynette Hunter** is a Professor in the School of English at the University of Leeds and currently Gresham Professor of Rhetoric.

**Nick Jeffrey** now teaches for the Open University and is a journalist. Active in civil rights in the South in the early 1960s, then in London docklands from the late 1960s, he later taught maths and coached football in Lewisham and Greenwich schools.

**Bruno Latour** is Professor at the Centre de Sociologie de l'Innovation, Ecole Nationale Supérieure des Mines, Paris.

**Jo Littler** is currently working on her PHD in the Graduate Research Centre in Culture and Communication at Sussex University.

**MAMA East African Women's Group** is a group of women from Somalia and other East African countries, meeting at the Gap Women's Centre in Sheffield to share stories which they also write and publish.

**Gerri Moriarty** is a Northern Irish community theatre practitioner/ teacher/ advisor. She has made several community plays dealing with issues of reconciliation in Belfast and recently worked with Jane Plastow on similar themes in Eritrea.

**Marie Mulholland** is former co-ordinator of the Women's Support Network in Belfast. She currently lives in Dublin.

**Okello Oculi** was born in Uganda, and currently lives in Nigeria. He has published three volumes of poetry and a novel.

**Rebecca O'Rourke** is a Lecturer in the School of Continuing Education at the University of Leeds. She was for several years an active member of the Federation of Worker-Writers and Community Publishers, with whom she retains strong links.

**Pragna Patel** is a founding member of Southall Black Sisters, an advice and campaigning group based in West London, and of Women Against Fundamentalisms. She has been active since 1982 around issues of domestic violence, policing and racism.

**Jane Plastow** is a lecturer in theatre studies and practitioner of theatre for development in Africa. Her work centres around issues of empowerment and giving a voice to marginalised people. She has worked extensively in Eritrea, Ethiopia, The Gambia, Tanzania and Zimbabwe.

**Jude Rosen** is a freelance writer and researcher and former academic who has written a novel on chronic disease.

**Rosie** is a Gypsy school girl who wrote her story in the context of a project of the Consortium of Traveller Education Services in Cleveland.

**Nira Yuval-Davis** is Professor of Gender and Ethnic Studies in the Department of Sociology, University of Greenwich. She is the author, among other titles, of *Gender and Nation*, Sage Publications, 1997.

**Mike Waite** helps edit the journal *Socialist History*, and has presented papers on 'flecks and carriers' in social movements at the annual 'Alternative Futures and Popular Protest' conferences in Manchester.

**Gregory Warren Wilson** is a professional violinist. His poetry has won many awards. His latest collection is *Hanging Windchimes in a Vacuum* (1997).

**Felicity Wyvern** lives in Norfolk, where she breeds snowy bantams. She has written poems all her life, but this is her first published poem.

**Michael Young** is a sociologist and social entrepreneur. Some of his poems, and those of his late wife, Sasha Moorsom, have been published as a book, *Your Head in Mine* (Carcanet, 1994).

# Space for co-existence?

We have put together this issue of *Soundings* at a time when ethnic hatred is again devastating regions and blighting lives in what was once, with care and difficulty, held together as Yugoslavia. And at a time, too, when NATO, on a mission of bringing to an end such violence across lines of difference, is pursuing its aims by bombing. The contrast between what we are trying to say here in this issue of *Soundings* and what is being done today in Europe - and in part in our name - is shocking.

The second half of this issue is devoted to the exploration of 'transversal politics', defined by Cynthia Cockburn and Lynette Hunter in their introduction as 'the practice of creatively crossing (and re-drawing) the borders that mark significant politicised differences'. How different from the ethnic cleansings of Milosevic, from the failure of 'the West' to see beyond the politics of partition, and from the violence which is asserted by both to be the only road to a solution. As Nira Yuval-Davis explains, transversal politics is an attempt to find a way of doing things which is neither the imposition of a single universal which refuses to recognise that there really are 'differences', nor the retreat *into* those differences as tightly-bound, exclusivist and essentialist identities. Neither Milosevic nor 'the Allies' in their various guises - which seem always to imagine the world in terms of drawing lines, dividing, allocating - remotely begin to recognise either these complexities or the political possibilities to which they might, just, give rise. And while in ex-Yugoslavia all sides pursue their aims by physical violence of various kinds, transversal politics experiments with talking, creative writing, theatre, joint projects. It would be naïve to argue, even to imagine, that the latter kind of politics could be simply transferred to the situation in the Balkans today. (Although it might be noted that one of the groups which contributes to the project of transversal politics is based in Bosnia, and brings together women of Bosnian Muslim, Bosnian Serb, Bosnian Croat and mixed backgrounds -

see also Cynthia Cockburn's photo-essay in *Soundings* 3.) But juxtaposing the two approaches throws into stark clarity the restricted terms in which 'our leaders' imagine the possibilities of international politics. And how can Blair condemn bombings in Brixton, Brick Lane and Soho, and Clinton the shootings in the Columbine school, when they themselves are 'solving' things through violence?

T he contributors to the transversal politics discussion would themselves not argue that they have a 'solution' to the difficulties of doing politics, of talking across differences. They recognise quite explicitly that this is tentative, experimental (although it is also suggested that some aspects of recent years' political dialogue in Northern Ireland - and granted the difficulties in which it is presently mired - 'have reflected the beginning of a shift in 'establishment politics' too towards transversal politics'). And this tone of exploration, of the recognition of difficulties, of the recognition and examination of failures, is again in shocking contrast to the performances we are forced to witness on what is called the world stage. Pragna Patel presents an account of her involvement in Southall Black Sisters which faces up to the difficulties which have been encountered, which tries to learn from failures, and which sees self-reflexivity as part of the very process of politics. Compare that with the assertive strutting of Robin Cook; the macho posturing, the refusal to admit the slightest doubt.

The danger of writing like this about experiments such as transversal politics is that they can come to seem almost bland or idealistic - that they may be arguing that if only we were nice to each other, and kept on talking, then all would be well. This is not how it is. As Nira Yuval-Davis argues, transversal politics does *not* assume that each and every conflict of interest is reconcilable. And here again the contrast with 'formal politics' is revealing. For while in Kosovo the Blair government interprets antagonisms as running so deep that they can only be solved by military intervention, back home here in Blighty his vision is of a politics which refuses to recognise real conflicts of interest at all - 'a politics without adversaries' as Chantal Mouffe put it in an earlier issue of this journal.[1] If anything is bland and idealistic, it is this. And while New Labour scatters the word 'community' through its documents and its pronouncements

1. Chantal Mouffe, 'The radical centre: a politics without adversary', *Soundings* 9, 1998.

without a thought for the complexities and conflicts which it is thereby covering up, transversal politics declares itself perennially sceptical about the term. It is precisely New Labour's bland official use of 'community' and 'multiculturalism' which can refuse to recognise, and in that lack of recognition thereby reinforce, the processes of marginalisation and oppression which cross-cut such unproblematised 'identities' .

These issues of the complexities of identities and differences are ones which have formed a continuing strand of reflection and debate within the pages of *Soundings*. Andreas Hess presented a position statement in issue 11; the theme of *Windrush Echoes* (issue 10) explored the negotiation of certain black and white identities in post-war Britain; the proposals for new forms of social settlement and public sector provision (*The Public Good*, issue 4) confronted issues of difference in the context of demands for 'universal' provision. The dismal horrors of the daily living-out of antagonisms are brought home in this current issue by Nick Jeffrey's detailed and thoughtful account of Stephen Lawrence's London.

I t may indeed be that this question of what Bruno Latour calls 'coexistence' is now more centrally on the agenda (or should be) than it has been heretofore. In his opening article for this issue, Latour argues that a key problem for any serious left party must be 'to explore coexistence between totally heterogeneous forms of people, times, cultures, epochs and entities'; that we must remodel the project of modernity away from the old universalisms and towards 'the new obligations of coexistence'. Once again, and as with the project of transversal politics, the aim must be - he argues - to reject both the more obvious, and opposed, alternatives on offer and strike out for something different. In this case the formulation is that we must reject both the current form of globalisation ('that is, in effect, Americanisation') and the reactive retreat into new localisms. Throughout his article, Latour is arguing for a reestablishment, and redefinition, of the differentiation between Left and Right (again, a proposition which clearly distinguishes this issue of *Soundings* from any form of Third Way politics); and key to this redifferentiation, he proposes, must be an exploration by the Left of the connections, rather than the oppositions, between locality and globality.

In this refusal to take as given currently dominant forms of economic globalisation Latour is also reflecting another of the continuing themes of this journal. And he is doing so too when he explores the basis on which such globalisation is justified. His fierce arguments against the division between a realm of (incontravertible, uncontestable) Science and a realm of Politics, and the imagination of economics as a Science, lying within the former realm (and being thus incontravertible too), precisely agrees with and develops the arguments we made in the Editorial to *Soundings* 10.[2] It is this removal of the economic from the realm of the political which enables the current form of globalisation to be presented to us as an inevitability. Economics must be brought back into the realm of the political; we must, in Latour's words, collectively appropriate the means of calculation.

One element which Latour brings to all these proposals which is rather newer to the pages of *Soundings* is that this task of reinventing modernity (which would be quite different from the 'modernising' proposed by Blair - the very difference itself undermining Blair's project by demonstrating that there is more than one way to 'modernise' ) is a task particularly appropriate to the Left in Europe. It is a proposal for a European Left, to set against a future of a world of untrammelled Americanisation (presumably aided by Blair), which is both extraordinarily attractive and, given what is happening in the south-eastern part of this continent, extraordinarily brave.

And not just 'far away' in 'the Balkans'. The crime against Stephen Lawrence was one among many; the London bombings shattered streets which in one way or another stood for some kind of coexistence. Latour argues that we are moving from an era when 'succession' most marked our political imaginations to one in which issues of simultaneous coexistence are more prominent. A move, he says, from time to space. Perhaps another way of putting that is to say that we have moved from an assumption that there was one grand History going on, to a recognition that there are in fact many. It could be argued that a real recognition of space throws into relief the existence of those multiplicities. Space in that sense is about simultaneity: co-existence.

It is also, of course, in part, the changing spatialities of our times which have made the potentialities and the problems of such coexisting multiplicities acute political issues in today's Europe. The combination of ethnic diversity and economic dereliction (two different aspects of two rather different periods of 'globalisation') in certain boroughs of south London is what Nick Jeffrey

---

2. Doreen Massey, 'I'm not an economist but ...', editorial, *Soundings* 10, 1998.

documents in his article. In contrast it has been pointed out by many a commentator that the bombs in Brixton, Brick Lane and Old Compton Street picked out with unnerving geographical precision locations which could each be seen, in different ways, as having a confidence in asserting a non-exclusive difference.

The women's projects in Bosnia, Israel, and Northern Ireland, in Southall, in Eritrea, and in all the other initiatives documented with such life under the theme of 'transversal politics' demonstrate, if cautiously, the necessity and possibility of continuing to assert such confidence. They also demonstrate that for new ways of 'doing politics' we must look somewhere else than Millbank and other such places; somewhere else than the excited small circles of advisors and journalists who - creating that self-referential circuit of debate, which so rarely questions its own terms or recognises just how tame and conservative it really is - occupy so much of our broadsheets, airwaves and television screens. In *Soundings* we have always recognised that 'the political' is far more than this.

*DM*

# Ein ding ist ein thing

## A (philosophical) platform for a left (European) party

### Bruno Latour

*Bruno Latour argues for a major revision of left thinking.*

The Fall of the Berlin Wall was supposed to render us all intelligent. Deprived of one arch-enemy, political reflection too could enjoy the 'benefits of peace' and stop making arguments, no matter how stupid, simply because they were expedient weapons during the Cold War. The forecast was that, in a more peaceful time, we should have become able to examine more quietly the inner quality of all these political philosophies the Left and the Right had thrown at each other for decades. The disarmament of arguments should have quickly followed the disarmament of weapons: swords should have become ploughshares.

Alas, in reading the prose of the present European leaders on the Left, exactly the opposite happens. Instead of the large diversity that was expected from more peaceful times, everyone of them speaks exactly in the same way as if we were still at war. 'Globalisation', 'freedom for the markets', 'deregulation', 'flexibility', 'information technology', they all say the same thing, without forgetting the new catchword: 'innovation'. After the Fall of the Wall, everything happened as if the Left parties alone had disarmed; as if they had been unable to profit from the changes of epoch to articulate in their own terms their issues and predicaments. Their discourse is that of their enemies, plus or minus a few changes. They are all vying for modernising the modernisation. No wonder that their voters have some difficulty in telling their Left apart from their Right and that they choose leaders by how youthful they look.

In the note below, I propose to reap the benefits of peace by reexamining some of the assumptions of the past fight between Left and Right, and by offering a very short ten point platform for reinventing another difference between Left and Right, a difference that will not inherit from the now defunct ones devised in the course of this century of Cold Wars. It will be, I am afraid, a very philosophical platform, and each argument will be simply sketched in order to keep within the time allotted to me.

## Plank 1: should we modernise the modernisation?

I am not sure a left party should advocate modernisation at all costs, as if more modernisation was still the order of the day. To be sure, the Left, in the grandiose scenography of the past, was associated with a thrust forward, with the great tale of Progress, with the arrow of time breaking free from the shackles of archaism to deliver us into an emancipated future. The problem is that times have changed so much that their ways of changing have themselves changed. If by the thrust forward is meant the idea that the future will be less entangled, less complex, less implicated than the past, this is clearly wrong. Only the Right can believe in a tale of Progress that means less regulation, less impediments, more freedom in the future than in the past. The only thing we can be sure of is, on the contrary, that whatever topic we choose to focus on, from ecology to genetics, from ethics to law, the future will be even more entangled than the past. There is still an arrow of time, it still goes forward, but it does not go from slavery to freedom any longer: it goes from entanglement to more entanglement. A left party would be well advised to come to grips politically with what has been captured by philosophers, journalists and thinkers alike under the vague and various words of postmodernity, reflexive modernity, hypermodernity. Whatever the words, something essential has happened in the way time flows, and the left parties cannot ignore it by trying to beat the Right at the great tales of Progress by simply pushing forward the youthfulness of their leaders as if the dispute was to decide who should modernise the modernisation faster. Maybe we have entered a different time than that of modernisation. It is time for a left party to engender a new difference with the Right on the way time flows and what the future will offer in terms of freedom and entanglement. To sum it up in one more provocative way, the quest for emancipation might no longer be the slogan of the Left.

## Plank 2: a special responsibility of Europe

Europe invented modernity, it has a special responsibility to, so to speak, disinvent it. I am not sure a left party should have the United States' worries as its one and only horizon. The United States is too powerful, too isolated, too insular in a way, to be interested in the specific European problems of remaking modernity. When manufacturers realise that one of their products leaves something to be desired, they do what is named a 'recall' of their products to fix, at their own expense, the problems and retrofits, the new devices that will make the product better. I believe that Europeans have to 'recall' modernity in order to turn it into a different project, especially a different way to tackle again the huge labour of universalising the world (see plank 5). This task will not be done by the United States which go on endlessly on the road of Progress, doing even more of the same, and still ignoring the consequence of their action, as if modernity was still the order of the day. No one seems to know exactly what it is to be European. Now the occasion arises to decide collectively what it is to be European: it is to have inherited the formidable project of modernisation and universalisation, and then, at the end of this century, to realise that something different is needed, that is, to disinvent it and deeply to modify its legacy. Just at the moments when there is much talk on the topic of globalisation, it is just the time *not* to believe that the future and the past of the United States are the future and the past of Europe. A left party should produce a new difference, utterly unrelated to the Cold War, between the future of the US and that of Europe. Actually, only the Left could imagine a European future, the Right - the neo-liberal one at least - can only imagine a universalist future, that is, in effect, an American one.

## Plank 3: from successions to coexistence

I have the feeling that we are slowly shifting from an obsession with time to an obsession with space. This is especially important for a left party, since it has associated so much of its energy and so many of its arguments around the notion of revolution, seeing reform as a disappointing and cowardly way of missing the call for revolution. Some people have argued that the Fall of the Wall marked the 'end of history'. If this means the end of events in history, this is plainly ridiculous, but if it means the end of an irreversible succession of epochs, each of them replacing the previous one and being replaced by the next through a sudden and radical revolution that leaves nothing but a blank slate, this 'end of history', like that of the end of modernisation, might be a profound insight. If, as philosophers argue, time is defined as the 'series of succession' and space as the 'series of simultaneity', or what coexists together at one instant, we might be leaving the time of time - successions and revolutions - and entering a very different time/space, that of coexistence. The key problem for a left party is no longer to 'make the revolution', nor even to substitute slow reforms for radical revolutions, but to explore coexistence between totally heterogeneous forms of people, times, cultures, epochs and entities. This is precisely what the Right is unable to do - even when it claims to be reactionary - since it goes on endlessly into a great narrative of revolutionary times - technical and economical upheavals - without being able to absorb the new obligations of coexistence. It is as if the Left had a duty of becoming 'reactionary' vis à vis these new Levellers who claim to prolong the continuous revolutions of the past. The Left should be able to say 'the time of revolutionary times has ended'. To the now empty dreams of revolutions, a left party would be faced with a completely unexpected (and truly 'revolutionary'!) task, that is of rendering coexistence possible on an Earth that no revolution can *simplify* any longer. During the Cold Wars, the only difference the Left could enforce with the Right was that of being 'for' revolutions. The new difference that could be elicited would be between an obsession with radical changes that eliminate the past for ever - now associated with the neo-liberal Right - and the new obligations of coexistence (that is the production of space), of heterogeneous entities no one can either simplify nor eliminate for good. Such a new distinction would also provide a clear-cut way for the new Left to distinguish itself, once and for all, from the old Ultra-Left, always lingering in the rear-vanguard of political action, and always agitating its red flags of total upheaval. There is no longer any Left left of the Left. The 'Ultras' are simply other types of reactionary revolutionaries.

## Plank 4: learning to live in a time of scientific controversies
A left party, it seems to me, is on the side of complication against the beautiful

simplification, the speedy shortcuts of the Right. In the recent past, that is in the times of modernisation, simplification was the order of the day, objects could be produced which had no unexpected consequences and that could replace older objects for good. The more science and the more technology was thrown in, the less disputes, so the idea went, would ensue. There was one best way, one economic optimum, one most efficient solution, means for ends. We are entering an entirely different playing field, because whatever we do we are expecting unexpected consequences. These many consequences (risks, unintended effects) feed back into the very definition of the objects. We are witnessing, so to speak, the revolt of the means. The completely unexpected feature for the Left is that science and technology do not simplify the discussions about objects any longer. Instead of extinguishing the political fires, they add fuel to the political, ethical and ecological controversies. This is why people like Ulrich Beck speak of 'risk society'. It does not mean a catastrophic version of society where the distribution of 'bads' will have replaced the distribution of 'goods', but simply this small and radical change that everyone can read about in the newspapers: science and technology add their uncertainties to the older ones, they do not subtract any. This creates an immense problem for the renewal of the Left because it has associated itself so much with science and technology. The Left knows fairly well how to expect more certainty from Science, but it has not learned yet how to thrive politically on scientific and technical controversies that it would much prefer to paper over. It is at this juncture that a left party could create a major new difference from the Right, by letting the Right go on in the traditional - and now deeply reactionary - call for more scientism, more acceleration of technology without discussion, less controversies, less regulation.[1] As in earlier times the mobilising slogan has been: 'No taxation without representation', the Left could revive this progressive call for action by chanting: 'No innovation without representation'. The time is gone when Science could be used to simplify the components of social order, to bypass politics. The Left should render life miserable to the simplifiers, to those who want to shortcut due process by kidnapping science and technology.

---

1.  When I use the words Science and Technology, I do not refer to what scientists and engineers and the rest of the collective do in laboratories but to the very specific politics of shortcutting politics invented by the West under the name of epistemology or philosophy of science.

## Plank 5: globalisation is not the order of the day

I am convinced that a re-established left party should be extremely careful with this term globalisation that has become the new catchword. As many anthropologists have shown, we are not entering a new globalised world characterised by the disappearances of cultures.[2] Exactly the opposite is happening, that is, the neoformation of many new cultures that subvert the very definition of what it is to be local and what it is to be global. We in Europe have invented, at some point, one idea of universality based on a certain version of a few peculiar sciences, and by comparison the 'local' was defined as exotic, odd, archaic and on a quick path to extinction. To the unity of global nature was opposed the multiplicity of local cultures. This is what happened when we were aiming at modernising the planet. But the two terms of that opposition between nature - in the singular - and cultures - in the plural - are being modified at once: the types of universalisation allowed by networks of scientific practices have lost the ability to render the other merely local by comparison; and the former 'locals' have invented, all around the world, especially through the new media of communications, new ways to make their difference heard and respected. This new 'globalisation of differences' (Appadurai) is exactly the opposite of the catastrophic scattering of incommensurable view points expected from the breaking up of modernisation. It would be a great pity if the Left, just at the time when the connections between local and global are utterly subverted by the rest of the planet, was finally embracing the repetitive mantra of globalisation and the 'new world order'. In addition, this would be a major political mistake, especially because, as has often been shown, the Right itself, everywhere in the world, is being split according to the now obsolete division between universality and locality: on the one hand, a neo-liberal Right that embraces globalisation, that is, in effect, Americanisation; on the other hand, a second Right, in reaction to the first, capitalises on the neoformation of cultures, and invents new ethnic localities, established on soil, blood and even genes. If there is one feature that could redifferentiate the Left from the two opposing Rights, it would be the exploration of the new connections between locality and globality that would, in addition, help Europe rework what it meant in the

---

2. A. Appadurai, *Modernity at Large: Cultural Dimensions of Globalization*, University of Minnesota Press, Minneapolis 1996.

past by modernisation and universality. No one else but the European Left will find that task so urgent, given the extraordinary diversity of Europe, and this fabulous entanglement of various contradictory universalities it finds itself built in and entangled with. In that respect, a new Europe shows a much more interesting type of future than the mere extension of America to the whole planet (plank 2).

These five first planks together define less a framework than a decor, so to speak, for the tiny platform on which I try to stand. It is extremely difficult to summarise them better in such a short time. They are just enough, I hope, to show that after the Wall has fallen, many chances to redifferentiate Left from Right have been missed that could be seized now, if only we redirected our attention to the new events. Sometimes it is difficult to detect what is contemporary. The Left, in my view, should not be like a disappointed heir who, after inheriting from the broken past of Cold Wars, would foolishly reject in disdain the brand new heritage that falls on it by happenstance, simply because it is not connected in any way to what was expected from its ancestors. Sometimes one can change ancestors or, as so often happens in genetics, discover that one inherits quite different traits from them. This is the historical change that should be seized on.

The five next planks are more substantial, but not easier, I am afraid, to summarise.

### Plank 6: one viable political order or two unviable ones

The Left has always had bad relations with Science - capital S - that is, with an epistemology unrelated to the real practice of the sciences that allows one to shortcut the political process. Instead of criticising and undoing this definition of science invented by its enemies, the Left, for more than a hundred years, has attempted to kidnap it for its own use. It has thus embraced without qualms this fabulous power: indisputable laws of society and economics, and even laws of history. Armed with this power that was not congenial to its real ancestry, it begot this monstrous beast that is responsible for so much misery: a scientific politics. The blood shed by this deadly association between science and politics is still on the hands of many people in the Left today. In spite of all the crimes committed by this idea that a science of society and a science of history could allow one to bypass due process, there still exist social scientists who believe they finally have gained the right to produce the ultimate scientific politics through the accumulation of enough 'symbolic capital'. Fortunately, now the situation has changed so much in the practice of science (plank 4), that the idea of a Science bypassing due process has changed camp entirely. It is now the Right which believes it has the right to shortcut political process because it benefits from the indisputable laws of one science, economics, that explains everything else provided the incontrovertible results of a few other sciences are thrown in as well - a bit of neo-darwinism, some 'eugenics', a few results of cognitive sciences (no matter if the real scientific disciplines that deal with life and brain offer totally different pictures). This shift in the appeal to Science is a great chance for the Left to elicit a new difference from the Right. The question has now become simple enough: do you want to build a political order with *two* chambers, the first one called Science capital S, that is said not to do politics but which takes all of the important decisions, and the other, called Politics, that is said to make the decisions but that is left with nothing but passions and interests? Or do you want, on the contrary, to build *one* due process where the questions of what ties all of us together, things and people, *Ding* and *Thing*, is explicitly tackled as politics? The first political order, with, so to speak, two attractors, is not viable and has produced a great many of the catastrophes of our age; the second, with only one attractor, is new but is to be experimented if we want to imagine a viable Body Politic. Because of its calamitous association with Science capital S, because of the crimes committed under the name of a Science of the laws of history, the Left has a special responsibility if it wishes to exist again and anew and to redifferentiate itself from the Right, to let science and technology be submitted or coterminous with due process, instead of being what bypasses the production of political order. This is especially important to fight those who, calling themselves the Greens, are trying, in the name of ecology, to reinvent one more avatar of the nightmarish scientific politic and who claim that they know, because of their Science and not because of due process, what counts and what does not count, who is important and who is not important in the great chain of beings. A new shibboleth, here again, could tell apart the Left from the Green: the Left lives under one political process of people and things, *Thing/Ding*, while the Greens still use the good old modernist two-attractor Body Politic. They want to save nature as a weapon against politics, the Left wants to save politics, so to speak, from nature. A new left party should be able to take up all of the issues put forward so diligently by the Greens, but to undo the double-bind that renders Green politics so inefficient.

## Plank 7: collective experiment

If the Left wishes to create a new difference between itself and the two Rights - the globalising right and the ethnicising Right - and also to distinguish itself from the Greens with their dual collectives of nature and society, it has everything to gain in registering a difference between Science and Research.[3] Given its past and the importance of science and technology, the Left should be strongly associated with the sciences and engineering, their development and innovations, but no longer with their politics of shortcutting politics. In other words, the Left has been associated with Science - and with catastrophic consequences - but not yet with Research. All of us have become parties in collective experiments on global warming, the influence of genetic engineering, conservations of species, demography, pollution, etc. We thus all have to practise something which, until recently, was the calling of very few specialists, namely *science policy*. Everyone now is led to practise science policy over a vast range of scientific and technical controversies. This has entirely modified the relations of the public with the producers of science and technology. We have to reorganise our polity accordingly. To be true to its glorious past of fighting on the side of *Aufklarung*, the Left does not have to embrace uncritically the call for industrialisation, modernisation, etc. If it wishes to fight obscurantism it can still do so, but the obscurity to be enlightened has changed shape. It is now the idea of collective experiments in which billions of people, animals and things are engaged, and wherein there is no protocol, no feedback loops, no debriefing, no archives, no monitoring, and no due process, that is no procedure to detect what has been learned and to decide what to do next. By moving from an association with Science, to an association with Research, the Left will have to wean itself from the secondary advantages that Science capital S give to its programme, the possibility of bypassing due process by appealing to incontrovertible laws. This has become impossible if the Left defines itself as what monitors a collective experiment, in which no shortcut is possible, to decide how many entities are going to coexist.

3. See a paper by the same author in *Science*, 10 April 1998.

## Plank 8: the collective appropriation of economic calculus

A different conception of science means, first of all, a different conception of economics. It is quite stunning to realise that after 150 years of left politics, political economy is still unexamined and uncriticised. To be sure, there have been many critiques of political economy, especially from the Marxist Left and former Ultra-Left, but, with the remarkable exception of Karl Polanyi, their goals have always been to *substitute* a more scientific economic theory for the ideologically tainted ones. In other words, the critique of political economy has always been done in the name of Science, that is of this extraordinary power to bypass political process in order to define better and faster the Optimum. I would be tempted to define political economy as what allows one to 'economise' politics; that is, literally, to shortcut its specific task, to save the social scientists from the incredible burden of producing collectively the calculation of the optimum. Political economics is the economy of politics. The Left has been obsessed, and still is, even when it dreams of reinventing itself, by the goal of 'appropriating the means of production'. But it has always been dramatically uninterested in the much more important task of collectively appropriating calculation. This is a great pity, since, for the new Left, a leftist science of economics is exactly as detrimental as a rightist science of economics. If, that is, by economics we mean this hardest of all social sciences which succeeds in the extraordinary double feat of being at once a *descriptive* Science without describing what it is that people practically do when being entangled with goods, and of being a *prescriptive* Science without paying the price of consulting all of those who are concerned in the calculation of the optimum. A double shortcut of the two hard travails of description - necessary for a legitimate science - and prescription - necessary for a legitimate ethics: that is indeed worth a careful critique. There is no way to shortcut the slow and painful composition of the whole collective simply by reading bottomlines on spreadsheets, no matter in which unit of account one does the calculation. Instead of embracing mainstream economics, or instead of dreaming of substituting a more scientific 'proletarian' economics for the 'bourgeois' one, the Left has the extraordinary opportunity to establish the first 'non-Marxist party' in the history of the West, that is the first party which does not believe in the slogan that one Science, economics, holds the laws of history and society.

## Plank 9: from calculability to descriptibility

The task for the Left is no longer to base itself on an alternative economics, but to ask the question again: is there a *successor* to economics, construed as this double bypass of description and prescription, of facts and values - facts in the name of values, values in the name of facts? I would be tempted to say that we might be shifting slowly from an ideal of calculability to a new idea of *descriptibility*. Calculations allowed the shortcutting of politics by ignoring all of the externalities that lie outside of the realm of what is to be calculated. Capitalism itself, in this view, is one among many of the powerful ways of distributing what is to be calculated - internalities - and what is not to be calculated - externalities. The limit of capitalism as a mode of calculation - not as a mode of production - is that it renders itself voluntarily very inefficient at calculating what it has left aside: unintended consequences, entanglement, due process, externalities. Actually, this is the only way to define itself as capitalism, as that which can extract itself from entanglement and allow someone to say confidently: ' we are quit', 'we do not have to deal with all of these other people, all of these needless entanglements'. Without the enormous task of limiting calculation - of which accounting and economics themselves are an integral part - without the formatting of all interactions into those two parts, what is and what is not calculable, neither appropriation nor capitalisation would be possible. The Left has thus an extraordinary opportunity, not in fighting capitalism as if it were a mode of production to which there was one and only one alternative (for instance another system of production), but in not pursuing economics at all, that is in not accepting that this strange double bypass invented in the eighteenth century to settle political order is the final word on what binds people and things together. The search for the optimum, or for the Good Life - this old definition of politics and economics - is not to be left to the Right using economics to shortcut description and prescription, but could be the object of a new political process that will sacrifice neither the task of description nor that of prescription. If there is one subject on which the Left may be true to its radicalness or cease to exist, it is that of reintroducing a new difference from the Right by insisting on finding a successor to economics as a way of organising the polity. The master Science of modernisation cannot be master in the new times that succeed modernisation. Instead of pursuing the vain hope of being agnostic in matters of theology, the Left might be well advised to begin at last to be agnostic in matters of economics.

What entangles people and things is still a complete mystery which the illusory mastery of political economy cannot even begin to fathom.

## Plank 10: a strong state

Everywhere in Europe, the remnants of the various old Lefts, in order to fight the cruelty of markets, are rallying to maintain what remains of former strong states that have been devised during the modern times. A new divide ensues between the Old and the New Left around the strange question of knowing if one should dismantle the state entirely or keep it as a buffer against the tides of globalisation. To rejuvenate themselves, leaders of the left parties are often trying to show that they can beat the Right at the game of dismantling the state faster than their competitors … Strange situation indeed that is inherited again from the various Cold Wars of this century. For the new Left to be invented, this is a caricature of a political debate. To be for or against the state, for or against the market, is no longer the criterion for deciding if a party is left or right. At least this is the sort of empty question from which the Fall of the Wall should have freed us. Markets, networks and institutions are ways of organising the types of attachments that people and things have with one another. There is no a priori privilege of one form of organisation over the other. The Left should be entirely agnostic vis à vis those forms and it should leave to the Right the extravagant commitment to one at the price of the exclusion of all the others. The Left should use another touchstone to decide which mode of organisation to use in specific cases: which one *increases* the ability to describe and to prescribe in the collective search for the optimum. If an institution allows us to go from ten powerful calculators to a thousand, then let's choose it: if, on the contrary, a pocket of market allows us to go from ten powerful shortcutters in the administration to a million consumers, then let's go to it. Yes, the Left should show its flexibility, by being indifferent to the *nature* of the organisations chosen. But it should be, on the other hand, obsessed by which one of these means of organisation increases the collective appropriation of the modes of calculating the optimum. Yes, the Left can be true to its urge to 'unleash the forces of production', meaning the forces of description and calculation, that is unleashing the forces of democracy. For those procedures to be in place so as to be able to choose collectively which mode of organisation is better, a strong state is indeed necessary, but that is not a state that substitutes for the ability of civil society to calculate and to reach the optimum. Yes, the state should be freed, freed, that is, from the burdensome task of substituting for the market and for the networks. The state, the new state of the Left, should be freed so as to concentrate on the only task no one else will do, that is to follow, document, debrief, induce, organise the collective experiment in which we are all, wittingly or unwittingly, engaged. This is a much better source of strength that the dinosaurian tasks of the past which aimed to replace the whole of civil society by shortcutting description and calculation. Only a strong state can make sure that the two Rights, the ultra Left, the Greens do not monopolise the collective calculations of the optimum, by their a priori Science of what binds all of us, things and people, together. Only a strong state could make sure that the collective experimentation is not aborted or bypassed.

I have said enough to show what should have become visible after the Fall of the Wall: never was there so much difference between the Left and the Right, contrary to what those who regret the 'good time' of the Class Wars say. In spite of the Cold civil Wars that took up so much energy, there has always been a deep agreement between the various Rights and the various Lefts on the urge for modernisation, on the inevitability of Progress, on the thrust forward of the arrow of time, on the call for emancipation in matters of personal mores, on the role of Science capital S as being to bypass due process, and, above all, on the infrastructural role of economy and on the continuous revolutions that would take place by irreversibly annihilating the past. For the first time, the Right and the Left can now part company on each of those items. I know that such a difference is not to be observed, it has to be produced, offered, experimented, elicited. In this brief paper, I have attempted to induce a new distinction between the Left and the Right, a much more radical one than simply vying for modernising the modernisation and pushing younger leaders to dismantle the welfare state faster. It can be summarised in a few words - although none, I agree, have any popular appeal: something else than modernisation is now at work in the world, and it offers a unique occasion for Europe and for the Left to re-establish themselves with a new pride. There is an arrow of time, there is energy to be unleashed, but it leads to coexistence rather than revolutions; emancipation, even in matters of personal life, might no longer be the order of the day; there is no way to shortcut political process any more, especially not through Science, especially not social science, especially not economics.

One last word on the author. I represent nobody and have no authority whatsoever to present this ten-plank platform for a party. I am simply a practitioner of the social sciences and I simply think that they have always been associated in the past with a political project. The question is to decide if this association is productive or not. In the expression 'social science', there are two words that do not work: the word social and the word social! Social scientists, in psychology, sociology and economics, have taken upon themselves, after the three English, American and French revolutions, to represent through their emerging sciences, the whole Society as one already organised Whole. This is what has given them the authority to speak in the name of the people who were manipulated, without them knowing it, by unseen forces which only the social scientists could detect and document. As Zygmunt Bauman has argued, they took it upon themselves to act as legislators. I don't believe that the task of social scientists is to substitute for the people by inventing an already existing Whole which would act as the hidden infrastructure of all their actions. I believe that people know pretty much what they do and that I, as a sociologist, have to learn from them what they do, and above all, what they say they do, not the other way around. A new association of the social sciences with politics would be possible if another definition of science and society was experimented with, and that is what I called above, a collective experiment. Neither the sciences nor the collective production of what binds people and things together can be shortcut by a Science and by a Society capital S. Instead of the social sciences, maybe something like 'political research' is in order, or better what Isabelle Stengers called 'cosmopolitics'. Before we invent the right mix of science and politics, my slogan will simply be: let us shortcut the shortcutters and see what happens.

*This article first appeared as a paper presented in Cologne to the fifth International Engineers' Conference of the Friedrich-Ebert Stiftung, in May 1998. The English text was published for the first time in the journal Concepts and Transformation, Volume 3, number 1/2, John Benjamins Publishing House, Amsterdam/New York 1998. We are grateful to the Friedrich Ebert Foundation for allowing us to publish it here.*

# The sharp edge of Stephen's city

## Nick Jeffrey

*Following the murder of Stephen Lawrence six years ago at a bus stop in South East London, his family's long campaign for justice has been a milestone in the battle against racism in Britain. Nick Jeffrey, who taught school and coached football in the area over the period of the campaign, reports from the band of estates in South East London where racism is still a large part of youth culture.*

I cycled slowly along the South Circular, past the sign 'Welcome to Greenwich - the Millennium Borough', then up the hill to Eltham Churchyard where I had seen, shortly after Stephen Lawrence was murdered, a graffiti 'WATCH OUT COONS, your now ENTERING ELTHAM'.

I remember such Jim Crow signs cursing entry to many American towns warning adult male 'negroes' not to be caught on the streets after sunset. In Eltham centre, mid-day or midnight, you see no black faces on the street. The Well Hall Road McDonalds opposite the churchyard has been a known hangout for racist youth, as was the Wimpy Bar before. It was on the wall of the church's graveyard that Derek Beackon's British National Party rally was cornered by anti-fascists, but from where they thundered their message of hate. That was 1991 and within two years three black boys had died in Greenwich of knife wounds - Rolan Adams, from a Thamesmead gang, then Rohit Duggal in Well Hall Road, the same road that Stephen died in. Seven other boys, four white, survived knife attacks in that period in Eltham, each incident with connections to the five main suspects in the Lawrence case, or to their alleged young racist associates. [1] It is that white flesh that even now is seen as providing legitimacy to the claim of one of the investigating officers into Stephen's murder, Detective Sergeant John Davidson, that it was ' ... not a racist attack. It was pure bloody minded thuggery'.

Police video surveillance a year and a half later showed four of the five suspects in the Lawrence case in Gary Dobson's flat, demonstrating how to plunge knives into black boys. [2] Here's Neil Acourt 'I reckon every nigger should be chopped up Mate and they should be left with nothing but fucking stumps' ; followed by Luke Knight: 'D'ya remember that Enoch Powell - that geezer, he knew ...' ; and later on David Norris: 'If I was going to kill myself do you know what I'd do. I'd go and kill every black cunt, every Paki, every copper, every mug that I know, I'm tellin ya ...' He and Neil's younger brother Jamie, inside at the time of the surveillance for another knifing, remain the prime suspects for Stephen's murder.

South from the Dome and along the edges of inner London are vast low-rise all-white council estates. Yards from the bus stop where Stephen was stabbed, a mixed race family had their home petrol bombed twice last year. Along these routes are a string of mixed-sex comprehensive schools, including the first two purpose-built in this country, for the postwar influx of tenants from slum clearances. The GCSE exam results published for that string of schools in Greenwich and Lewisham are among the lowest in the country for attaining five grades A to C; at 10 per cent they are half the 20 per cent which is cited by Ann Power as the average for the 13 similar riot estates she studied.[3] Truancy rates are high. Bullying and gang violence have been major issues. The drift between boys' and girls' results is among the highest in England. Half of the English education authorities where boys' achievements is 25 per cent or

1. Stephen Lawrence Inquiry (henceforth 'Inquiry'): 'Closing Submissions of Counsel, William Panton, representing the London Borough of Greenwich' , 7.9.98, *The Stephen Lawrence Inquiry; report by Sir William Macpherson*, 2.99,CM 4262-1 (henceforth the *Report*), pp38-39.
2. The Stephen Lawrence Inquiry-Appendices, 2.99,CM 4262-II (Revised) (henceforth the *Appendices*), Appendix 10.
3. Anne Power & Rebecca Tunstall, *Dangerous Disorder: Riots and violent disturbances in thirteen areas of Britain 1991-92*, Joseph Rowntree Foundation, York 1997.

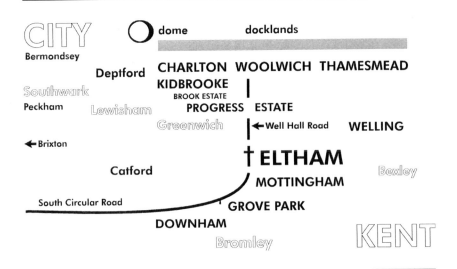

less on the exam measure are those directly to the west and north of Greenwich - a real south and east London belt of young male failure, black and mainly white. With one exception - in Plymouth - the other half of such authorities are all in the north of England. The disaffection of white boys, the rise of youth gangs, and the resurgence in racially motivated violence stretches along these routes. It does not stop at the oft-pilloried Tudor gates of Eltham. It is seamless from Thamesmead, Stanley Kubrick's setting for his self-banned *Clockwork Orange*, down through the grim outer parts of Lewisham into Bromley.

The Downham Estate, at the southern end of this stretch, is one of England's biggest. Here from May to October 1996 no buses ran after six. Companies withdrew all six routes, serving 30,000 people, because of muggings, hijackings and assaults on drivers - especially black drivers. These were the work of gangs of white boys aged eleven to fifteen. [4] In February last year Allison Moore, a young black teacher at a primary school in Catford, was attacked and seriously hurt while working late at school, being cursed as 'black bitch' by four white boys aged about sixteen. Children from that school go on to attend secondary schools in Downham, and that is where Allison lived. In

---

4. *News Shopper-Lewisham and Catford*, 15.5.96 & 22.5.96.

March her home was invaded by one balaclava-ed man, while another painted swastikas and 'NF' outside. She had also received death threats. The NF denied involvement, though they had focused on her school in 1994 election leaflets. Near this house (from which Allison has now moved), a new black-led self-build co-operative housing project suffered four arson attacks in four years, with the loss of two houses, which they rebuilt. 'NF' was daubed on buildings.

Here along these same bus routes from Downham up to Eltham, six years back, young black children were regularly set upon while awaiting a bus home. Events following the murder of Stephen had a galvanising effect along these routes. Suddenly black dads and we teachers guarding bus stops were backed up by police. Road tax crackdowns were suddenly and effectively turned on the racists. Troublesome, dangerous tenants were moved with haste by Lewisham. Greenwich followed suit. By 1994 violence had become such an issue that industrial action by teachers was threatened as a last resort if the most violent kids were not excluded.

In the 1990s gangs of white schoolboys aged 11 to 16 grew up across the area - excluded, truanting, or even working within schools. They established a gang culture in Thamesmead to the east, in Eltham along Well Hall Road, but especially in the south in Mottingham and Downham, all linked across borough boundaries. In that culture it was normal to be racist - adults referred to it as normal teenage male expression. At their then Mecca - Millwall Football Club - the gangs were ranked. (Charlton Football Club, who had no local ground over that period, did not provide such a focus for the gangs.) Boys were arrested repeatedly for hijacking, joyriding, torching and for 'porking' Asian-owned shops. Isolated Asian families suffered harassment from teen and younger boys through theses areas.' Lee told me, 'we just go and do another job and get nicked again. Then our case, when it next comes up, is just put off again, so's the next one can be what they say - "taken into account"'. By 1996 certain boys in Downham were targetted and given curfews and area exclusion orders as conditions of police bail. They were geographically excluded from within 500 metres of their secondary school, and some of them from Grove Park Station, which they had captured, hijacking a train. These curfews and exclusions were a first in England and were a local initiative. Shadow Home Secretary Jack Straw was invited to see, and was followed by

Michael Howard himself. Those gangs peaked and broke in 1996. But according to police, in January last year they had resurfaced as local nuisance groups. The following month, on the gangs' home patch, Allison Moore was attacked.

Greenwich Action Committee Against Racist Attacks (GACARA) has kept regular statistics of racial victims over those six years. Greenwich Police have joined a Joint Racial Incidents Unit with Greenwich Council and provide their own statistics based on recorded incidents (changed since the April 1998 audit to count victims as well as incidents). There have been some differences in the sources and statistical methods for recording the attacks, but all the figures show an unacceptably high, and continuing, level of attacks. GACARA recorded 1013 for 1996. Attacks resulting in bodily harm had, according to both sources, decreased since the 1993 murder - until 1997. Night attacks on property have increased since 1996 and arson has become an increasing concern. Catford Police statistics for neighbouring Downham show similar trends. And there remain unsolved murders. Only one boy was convicted for the murder of Rolan Adams, although he was attacked by a gang. A strawberry blond boy mentioned by witnesses to Stephen's murder has never been identified. Of the five accused of Stephen's murder, three were acquitted. Prime suspects Jamie Acourt and David Norris have not been tried. The Crown Prosecution Services withdrew charges on them citing inconsistent identifications. Stephen's friend Duwayne Brookes, who was with him that night at the bus stop, was discredited as a prime witness by police actions and the CPS. Why so remains a question. It was at Duwayne that 'What?... What, nigger?' was shouted that night. He escaped, but remains a victim. The picture that emerges is one of widespread incidences of racism and racist attacks, coupled with an inadequate response by the authorities. The Inquiry, set up to investigate the policing of the murder, found incompetence, and considered alleged corruption through the Norris criminal links; they found, rather than individual racist officers, institutionalised racism in the Met.

## An imperial context

The pretty mock-Tudor estate where Stephen Lawrence died was purchased by the Royal Arsenal Co-op in 1925 and renamed the Progress Estate. It had been built for Arsenal munitions workers in 1915 by the War Ministry, and had a garden city lay-out of 1200 houses, designed by Sir Frank Baines, architect of many popular LCC estates. There is a history in the area of heavy industry, of work in the docks, on the railways and in military-related industries - and of highly-organised working-class institutions. The Arsenal once employed 80,000. These other estates from the interwar period housed the families of workers from skilled trades such as building and print, as well as heavy industry and transport. The 'deserving' tenants, from clearances up in Bermondsey, were all white. The job losses for these communities have been massive. The closure of the AEI electrical engineering works in 1968, a sudden loss of 8000 jobs, was a portend, followed by closure of docks and of engineering industries. This blighted an area built for the industries of an imperial power to house the necessary labour power, later expanded to cater for the demands of a politically strong labour force - even after reproduction of that labour power ceased to be an economic necessity.

Thirty years back, when extra funds were allocated by Wilson's Labour government for Education Priority Areas, two-storey estates with gardens didn't feature in their designated areas of social need. In fact, such housing was used as a measure of prosperity and achievement. How wrong they always were. Male unemployment has remained high across these estates to the south, keeping steady at over 20 per cent for a generation. Dads no longer had jobs with apprentice openings for boys. Male expectations collapsed and the scope for boys narrowed. Those bus hijackers were not, as some professors of education have proclaimed from on high, the illiterate and innumerate. The boys in the top gangs were, in my experience, bright kids who often entered secondary school with some achievements and initial interest. The girls fare better - work harder - and have attained more skills, from IT to personal communication and presentation. The restructuring of the local economy has been harder for boys to cope with. They are afraid. They feel bottom of the heap, yet still need the male display which frightens others.

Housing sons and daughters near their parents in pursuit of sustaining communities, suggested by many sociologists, was for a long time policy in Greenwich, as in Bermondsey. Large parts of those areas thus remained white, and for blacks became no-go areas. A generation back, West Indian families living to the west, in areas such as Peckham or Brixton, began sending children out to what were seen as safe suburban schools, away from the influence of aspiring yardies and gangstas and the attentions of police. They next wanted to move out into these suburbs, where the only significant ethnic minority presence was Asian shopkeepers around the older Woolwich town centre. Simon de Banya operates the Black Information Network's website BLINK, where Stephen Lawrence Family Campaign items can be viewed. Simon says, 'Greenwich for black people is the racist capital of London ... Eltham is seen by many blacks as a fortress Eltham, and some suggest that it could be seen as a front line beyond which a white Kent is the retreat ... we know of racist families from Greenwich and Lewisham who have bought houses in some of those towns and moved out. These are not just deprived families from those estates, but well-off people, involved in racism, and there's nothing to stop them getting mortgages.' The reputation of Eltham has suffered - it is regarded as racist, supposedly breeding racists, now harbouring them.

Eltham was given nationalist kudos - and young racists a certain legitimacy - by the proximity and volume of the BNP 'bookshop' in nearby Bexley. Five of England's largest pubs, from Downham to Thamesmead, have been the habitual meeting places of the BNP and NF, each one closed for violence. The Yorkshire Grey at Eltham Green, once host to Blood and Honour, and Combat 18, is now yet another McDonalds. The NF logo, however, remains the graffiti of choice - it has more punch and is easier to scratch into a textbook. In 1990 'NF' was painted 3 feet high at the Orchards Youth Club next to the estate. Neal Acourt was excluded for that, along with David Norris. [5] (The only suspect who was actually accused of direct contacts with racist or fascist movements was Gary Dobson, and that was put to part two of the Inquiry, without the accused being present. [6])

## Routes of racism and roots of racism

'Wall of silence ? ... much of it [information] was not anonymous and the bulk of it came from within the local population ...'

*Michael Mansfield, QC for the*
*Lawrence Family, on leads to the killers*

The Macpherson Inquiry revealed that 26 different people from within the area gave evidence implicating the five main suspects in the case within two weeks. Fourteen of those residents were known to the police. Three were police. If these were followed up, the evidence has gone missing. The five were named by nine different sources, three of those with more than adequate evidence and reason for arrest within 24 hours.[7] They were observed but not arrested until two weeks later. They were even photographed removing probable forensic evidence but this was not followed up. The 'wall of silence' appears to have been a police construct, aimed at deflecting accusations of racism from the police and onto the 'community' of Eltham. The police officers wanted it both ways - that it wasn't a racist crime, and that it was a crime supported by a racist community. They have now been exposed, unable to maintain either position. Nevertheless there still remain key witnesses, such as 'K' , whose friend 'Grant' went to the police, was first ignored, and then later would not testify. [8] This young and curious skin went to the Acourts' house shortly after the murder and observed four of the gang cleaning up. 'B', who witnessed the murder from the bus, was dismissed as a 'Walter Mitty'. Others did feel intimidated by the gang and their family connections. But an entirely silent community? After 88 witnesses and 10,992 pages, we now know the answer is no.

One of the five main suspects, Norris, lived away from the estate, in a large walled house out near Bromley. His father Clifford was for years known to all local police for drug and gun running and intimidation of witnesses. The Acourts and Norris were connected through relatives named Stuart.[9] These roots in the infamous Southeast London criminal diaspora make the families atypical of local estate gangs. They all went to the same youth football clubs - which in South East London usually involve parents as well. Three attended the ex-ILEA flagship school Crown Woods at Eltham. Norris was excluded from Cooper's School in Bromley in 1989 for uncontrollable disruptive behaviour and attended a special school.[10] Neal Acourt's and Gary

---

5. 'Inquiry', transcripts of hearings, Michael Mansfield QC, 29.6.98.
6. 'Inquiry', Part Two, submission of *Searchlight*, from September, 1998,p.3., refuted in *Searchlight*, October 1998, p3. (Part Two of the Inquiry took evidence beyond the Stephen Lawrence case, locally and nationally.)
7. *Report*, chapters 13 & 33, *passim*. *Appendices*, Appendix 5, transcript of evidence of day 2, Michael Mansfield QC, 24.3.98.
8. 'Inquiry', Final Submissions with regard to Part 1 on behalf of Mr & Mrs Lawrence, Michael Mansfield QC, pp21-22, appendix 1, p33, appendix 2, pp40-46.
9. *Loc.cit*, p24. ; 'Inquiry', transcript of hearings, Michael Mansfield QC, 29.6.98.
10. *Loc.cit*,. 30.6.98.

Dobson's GCSEs approached at Crown Woods, Jamie transferred from there, joining Luke Knight at their local Kidbrooke School for a fresh beginning to his own GCSE's in January 1991. In June he was said to have threatened a black boy named Dean Holgate with the replica Smith and Wesson handgun behind the gym. In September he was in a fight with a black boy named Sean Kolitis. After five days exclusion white and black gangs fought outside the school gates. The next day Jamie was excluded again for carrying a monkey wrench, and the next month permanently expelled. [11] The Acourts and associates, finished with schooling, styled themselves The Krays. Many referred to them as The Untouchables. Although popular among whites in school, they were deeply unpopular on the estate. Why did no-one ever pick up, identify and deal with this two-to-three-year build-up of hate and violence, which peaked in Stephen's death?

The five have been portrayed in the media as either vicious and angry, as when escaping the Inquiry, or as arrogant and disdainful (within the Inquiry), or as skins. Not the full story. They affect a slick clubbish image. They dress well and can look good. Neal Acourt expressed on the Police surveillance video a distaste for skinheads, and disappointment with the BNP for depending on skins: '... all these straight bods, they wanna vote for them mate, but they see all these fuckin yobbo fucking skinheads and they think, "who wants to vote for them?"'.[12] Today they attend local clubs and pubs, and Jamie, always the decent footballer, plays on Southeast London pitches.

The Lawrence family lived in nearby Woolwich. After the murder Stephen's mother went with her sister Cheryl Sloley to the local Sainsburys. Recognised by a white woman in the car-park, Cheryl was told, 'If he hadn't been here, he would still be alive'. To Doreen Lawrence this meant' if he wasn't in this country, he would still be alive'. Five years on, there was a silence in court following the telling of this story.

The cast bronze plaque set in the paving where Stephen died has been subjected to many atrocities - with swift response from Greenwich's anti graffiti unit. From the plaque a pretty white-walled path passes under the Tudor-style terrace leading to a village green which could grace a travel brochure. For

---

11. *Loc.cit.* 29.6.98.

Christmas 1997 the walls proclaimed 'EEDL - the Eltham English Defence League'. Fright is fact. Planning Professor Peter Hall told me before the Lawrence inquiry that such' hatred and complicit silence would fly in the face of Alice Coleman's theories of good estate environment leading to good social behaviour'.

Roger Hewitt and his field researchers from the Institute of Education at London University found 'wall-to-wall racism' among youth while interviewing following the murders of Rolan Adams and of Rohit Duggal. On the night of the murder, while Stephen lay bleeding, four youth cruised up and down Well Hall Road, laughing loudly from their battered red Astra.[13] Five years later we learned that days passed before these lads were traced, and that some were among those implicated in the Adams murder. How they knew on the night what had happened remains a question.

Perhaps there are literal Routes of Racism along these bus lines and along this bush telegraph of graffiti messages. That is the title of the booklet Hewitt did for the Greenwich Racial Equality Unit.[14] Hewitt transforms this into a search for roots. Such routes provide actual connections, effective only where there are already roots of racism, which he argues is a social construct. He and colleagues looked at tags, listened to jokes, listened at clubs and schools, asked about families, estates, and football. They argue that the social construct of racism is learned, reinforced by experiences and by some stories and myths.

Football plays an important part in this culture of racism. Youth football is big and was once white. Following the 1981 Brixton riots, more inner-city clubs were formed and boys in them had to travel out for competition and for pitches. I managed Tulse Hill, a Brixton and Peckham club. When we travelled to Greenwich, racial abuse was common on and off the Sunday pitches. I recall boys of the same age as the Acourts trying at age ten to attack visiting players. Later the Acourts' club, Samuel Montague, began to attract racists. They expelled Neil Acourt in 1991 for a post-match knife threat allegedly against a black boy from Red Lion, a Peckham and Deptford club.[15]

---

12. *Appendices*, Appendix 10.
13. *Report*, sections 11.35,16.18,38.13, & ch 20 *passim*.
14. Roger Hewitt, *Routes of Racism: the social basis of racist action*, Trentham Books, Stoke-on-Trent, 1996.
15. 'Inquiry', transcripts of hearings, 29.6.98.

Acourt's brother, Norris, and Knight all left as well. I often thought that the skill of our black boys was seen as a threat to some white boys and their dads, a threat beyond the football pitch. This seemed particularly so on the sensitive subject of school district team selection. The cultures of racism are particularly embedded in the Sunday leagues, where parents are also part of the club. Brian Clarke, Secretary of the London Youth Football Association, told me, '... even from the FA's 1991 survey, 80 per cent of youth football was Sunday. This has surely increased since, with the decline in school football and the declining popularity of youth clubs in general. We seem to have less open racism now than in the past, but maybe it's disguised. We do take up more disciplinary actions on racism than before, and have adopted anti-racism in our charter for quality.' The Bexley and District Youth football league is England's biggest and most powerful Sunday league: it stretches as far west as Brixton, and has 8000 players, 480 teams. Brian Miller, Chairman of that league, told me, 'Club representatives will raise objection even now to applications from inner city [i.e. Brixton and Peckham clubs] ... Now with so many ethnics, it is no longer such a surprise to see two or three black players in many teams. Certainly things appear better, but it's still the parents who are the problem I think.'

Years back you could hear 'black cunt', with no apology offered for racism; now 'black cunt' will be justified as being no different from calling a player, say, an 'Irish cunt', and will be defended as not at all racist. Hiding behind words is the current state of multi-culturalism on the pitches. From 1988 I managed school and District football in the area, selecting mixed teams from all Greenwich and Lewisham secondary schools. I had to confront skin dads loud with racial abuse from the touchlines. I once thought that these beliefs were merely handed down by adults. But my view changed while working eleven years in these schools. The parents of racist boys are not necessarily racist themselves, but in many cases are anguished about it. I recall those who came to talk about it.

There are roots to the racism which are not grafted on, but are nurtured in a culture owned by these youth, created by them and based in their own experiences, including an overwhelming sense of being discriminated against. The boys feel bottom of the heap. They experience conditions which they perceive as racism against themselves and their families. They see this in school and in sport, in music and dress and other cultural symbols, in their family's housing and the job market, even in policing. They see it in reference to their imagined community. Enoch Powell's notorious Rivers of Blood speech of 1968 - '... their homes and neighbourhoods changed beyond recognition, their plans and prospects for the future defeated...' - has been quoted by singer Billy Bragg as 'putting a knife in the hands of Stephen Lawrence's killers'.

Outside the Eltham dole in 1994 was a large graffiti, 'hang the Catford 27' - an allusion to the alleged rape of two white girls behind the old Catford McDonalds, at the time a rendezvous for wannabee young yardies and gangstas. The police did not prosecute anyone for this offence. The white boys took their own message from this. This incident is a likely source for David Norris's videoed display: 'I would go down Catford and places like that, I'm telling ya, I'd take two sub machine guns and I'm telling ya, I'd take one of them, skin the black cunt alive mate, torture him, set him alight ... I'd blow their two legs and arms off and say "Go on you can swim home now"'. [16]

In 1992 in Kidbrooke next to Eltham, a white boy - a former classmate of Jamie Acourt's but not racist - went out to buy his mum some cigarettes. One of the black boys from the Kidbrooke School confrontations with Jamie Acourt was on the street with a gang. The white boy was beaten up. The attacker wasn't punished, and another story of non-punishment of black boys spread. That story didn't say that the next day the victim played for me in goal - with swollen black eyes and lips - for Inner London Schoolboys against Essex in the county finals. Most of the goalkeeper's team mates were black and they nominated him man of the match.

Black boys are perceived by white boys as getting away with more in schools, the last place injustices should be tolerated. Some white boys think that black boys avoid being excluded for actions which would bring exclusion for them. Stories of sexual assaults in schools, by groups of black boys, on girls and even on female teachers, abound, usually as examples of non-punishment. Teachers are seen as being afraid of certain black lads or as being without the backup of authority should they attempt to discipline them. Racism is fertilised through the policy dog being regarded as having bite in

16. *Appendices*, Appendix 10.

one direction and a blind eye in the other. My student 'Jason' was in a fight with 'Dwayne'. 'Jason' got a suspension and parents called in for discussion. 'Dwayne' didn't. 'Jason' was angry. 'That misses Hawkes put that down in the racial incidents book and it wasn't. I mean it was a fight, just that. So why doesn't Dwayne cop it?'. When white boys experience what they feel to be an injustice, they often see it in racial terms. What is wanted is a fair cop. Clothing symbols are also experienced as discrimination. Another of my students,' Gary, had his jacket with the Union Jack on it confiscated from school . He told the headteacher: 'What is this? What about those Jamaican flags on jackets? Are you afraid to take those?' Too often in these cases, there is simply punishment, and the aim of schooling - education - is lost, with more seeds of prejudice sown.

Roger Hewitt reports that past policies in Greenwich were implemented '... in ways that did more to demonstrate the school's anti-racist stance than to assert the underlying principles of justice and fairness'. Many boys move from all-white primary schools to mixed secondary schools whose multicultural programmes are not always well-conceived; and for them it can feel like a further put-down to have a celebration of what they see as foreign cultures, while being denied a Britishness with its imperial history of plunder, pillage, slavery and murder. Royal Navy and Artillery and Arsenal leave powerful and old architectural symbols in Greenwich.

Ian Macdonald QC represented Stephen's friend Duwayne Brookes in the Lawrence Inquiry. Macdonald led the Inquiry into the 1986 murder of Ahmed Iqbal Ullah in a Manchester school playground. In his report, *Murder in the Playground* [17] he argues:

the fundamental error ... of morally based anti-racist policies is that they assume that a complicated set of human relations, made up of many strands, including class, gender, age, size,....race, can be subsumed into a simple white versus black pigeon hole. It is the problem of white versus black that (then) has to be dealt with. The other things are assumed and not dealt with. This simple model assumes that there is

---

17. Ian Macdonald, *Murder in the Playground- the Burnage report*, Longsite Press, London, 1989, p.348.

uniform access to power by all whites, and a uniform denial of power to all blacks. Clearly this is not the case. We do not believe that an effective anti-racist policy can exist unless the other issues are dealt with, in particular class and gender.

## Fin de siecle in justitia?

The Lawrence family soon perceived that it was racist attitudes while Stephen bled that allowed delays in emergency treatment, and that encouraged delays in investigating the suspects, while the police pursued questions about Stephen himself. This was in spite of the fact that Stephen was not into gangs or drugs. He was finishing his A-levels, aiming for a university place in architecture for which he had excelled in work experience. He was a top athlete and an active Methodist. But no cop ever went to ask questions of all those teachers and coaches and ministers who held him in high esteem. Doreen Lawrence emphasised '... he did not distinguish between black and white, he saw people as people' . Following on the Lawrence family campaign, the 'Bad Apple' theory of police racism, the only definition accepted by the Scarman Report following the 1981 Brixton riots, is at last to be supplemented by a recognition of institutionalised racism in the police. This is a major achievement of the Lawrence family and their supporters, although it remains to be seen how the metropolitan police will act to deal with the problem.

In spite of the achievements of the Lawrence campaign, there remain many lesser-known examples of attacks on black people, solved and unsolved. Reports of three similar street deaths of young men in London in the past year were submitted to the second phase of the Inquiry. The black teacher Allison Moore remains injured, and her beating unsolved.

The sign now on the South Circular into Eltham reminds you that it is 'time for GREENWICH 2000'. The Stephen Lawrence Family Campaign have called for the Millennium Commission to support Justice 2000, a campaign which, as Simon de Banya says, aims 'to end the millennium in Greenwich without blood on the hands of this society... there are unsolved murders of black boys, and murders which even when solved remain unprosecuted'. The Millennium Commission, however, says Simon, have stayed clear of this campaign, and they remain distant. Nevertheless, as the Stephen Lawrence Campaign has shown, campaigning can achieve change. As Allison Moore told her children, 'You all know the bullies can not win.' Hundreds overflowed the rally in Downham in her support and against racism. The memories of that meeting will surely focus on 11-year-old Shona Sloley, Stephen Lawrence's cousin, who attends Crofton School in Catford. She read from her letter to Allison, 'think of me. I think of you.' Later in the month, exactly five years after Stephen's murder, a candlelit vigil was held by 300 people over the spot where he died, led by Bishop for Stepney John Sentumu, who was one of the three advisors appointed to the Judicial Inquiry. For the second time in the month a chorus of hundreds singing 'We Shall Overcome' swelled these routes. Neville Lawrence proposed a Stephen Lawrence Educational Trust, 'to open up avenues for other young people to study and achieve'.

Efforts to combat racism are also being made by Greewich Borough. Harcourt Alleyne of the Greenwich Racial Equality Unit told me, 'We would support Roger Hewitt's view that policies based in moral admonition or in guilt and accusation will cut no ice, will more likely bring backlash.' Hewitt's team and Greenwich Council, through schools and youth clubs, are seeking ways to avoid that. They seek to understand how these youth view their own disadvantage and injustice, and they seek a vision of identity that is not the British bulldog. Football, theatre and music are points of entry - plus girls. Hewitt says 'Girls who are not racist could be very critical of the racism ... of what they regarded as the cowardly behaviour of boys ... one area of hope ... lies in discovering what enables these ... girls to stand apart.' Tim O'Shodi of the Downham self-builders explained to me that, 'the kids drawn into racism are without their own hope and desires, and that is what must be opened to them'. The boys are afraid of failure. What is the easy route to avoid being labelled failure? To not try or not be seen to try. This stance is draped around classrooms, even sports pitches. 'Yeh I might've gotta trial at Charlton, but I couldn't be bovered', offered 'Jed', who was my student. A culture is produced from among boys which, by defining their own terms and agenda, edits out failure. This gives them a certain control.

The Greenwich Racial Equality Unit has taken this up. Yazim Patel, employed in the field, explains, 'the programme is now based at Charlton

Athletic FC at the Valley and we are extending it into youth clubs, employing youth workers and coaches. This is part of the FA's Kick Racism out of Football campaign'. Millwall, once the main venue of racist thugs in Southeast London, pioneered such efforts in the 1980s. You now can see blacks sitting in the New Den, but rarely at The Valley. Last August Charlton announced that the five Lawrence murder suspects 'would not be welcome' at the Valley. Greenwich and Lewisham Councils have finally passed 'quality controls', which require all clubs to adopt anti-racist policies as a condition for pitch bookings. However, it has to be said that these policies are not going to reach the parts which need reaching. It is Sunday league clubs which are the thriving heart of Southeast London youth culture, and few of these remain as youth clubs: most are now private clubs. Since ILEA was closed, councils have been selling sports grounds. Brian Miller, of the Bexley and District league, reveals, lots of these big clubs have now bought into their own grounds, or at least bought long leases, so the council pitch letting policy won't affect them'. This is big territory and the Kick Racism Out campaign has a lot of work to do before much ass is kicked.

There is a continuing difficulty in defining the problem. 'Inner-city' is not a term that describes the problems I have been discussing. Who defines a crisis? Only when social relations of production are broken, when control of property and territory is endangered where it matters, to those who matter, will education and youth be considered a crisis by those in power. Isolated, area-based, urban policies don't come anywhere near to addressing the political economy of race, culture and class.

In spite of the problems, though, there are grounds for hope, largely stemming from the campaigning work of black and anti-racist groups. I finish with a quote from Michael Mansfield QC, from his opening speech on behalf of the Lawrence family:

Nearly 50 years ago from now, namely in 1948, in the Southern States of America, there was a black Baptist minister by the name of Dr. Vernon Johns, and his parish was a Baptist church in Dexter, Alabama. Following a series of murders of young black men in that town in 1948 and just before, by gangs of white men, those murders having gone unchecked, with no sanction, and in the face of enormous public disapproval and the risk of violent retribution, he entitled his last sermon, 'It is safe to murder Negroes'. He was detained by the police and forced to leave. He did. His successor was Dr. Martin Luther King, and hence the birth of the Civil Rights movement in the United States of America.

# The Stephen Lawrence Charitable Trust

Stephen Lawrence's ambition was to study and practice architecture. The Trust established in his memory will provide other young black people with the opportunity to study architecture and other associated arts. Students will be encouraged to study in the UK, the Caribbean and in South Africa. Established in August 1998, the objects of the Stephen Lawrence Charitable Trust are:

To advance the education of the public in the art and science of architecture by any means which is charitable, and in particular but without prejudice to the generality of the foregoing, by the presentation of an annual Memorial Lecture in the memory of Stephen Lawrence.

To advance education by the provision of scholarships and bursaries or maintenance allowances to any person the Trustees deem fit, provided that such persons are undertaking (or are about to undertake) a course of formal education at any university or other recognised educational establishment to prepare or assist such persons to gain entry into the profession of architecture.

BECOME A FRIEND OF THE STEPHEN LAWRENCE TRUST

- Make a donation as an individual, organisation, company or trust.
- Make a one-off donation of £250 (minimum) by Gift Aid - we can recover the tax which will increase your gift by one third.
- Make a covenant to the Stephen Lawrence Trust by a Banker's Order drawn regularly over 4 years.
- Give long term support by leaving a legacy.

Cheques should be made payable to:
THE STEPHEN LAWRENCE CHARITABLE TRUST.

THE STEPHEN LAWRENCE CHARITABLE TRUST
9th Floor, 16 Palace Street, London SW1E 5JD
Tel: 0171 963 4406  Fax: 0171 963 4440
e-mail: beverley@tgwu.org.uk
Website: stephenlawrencecharitabletrust.org.uk

*Trustees:* Doreen and Neville Lawrence, Tim Cook, Ros Howell, Elvin Oduro, Jon Snow, Arthur Timothy
*Registered No.* 1070860

# Five poems

## The Point, the Turning

Each night you turn away from me to sleep,
as if sleep were some intimacy you felt
more privately than anything you feel for me.

We share the quilt, this dark, occasional dreams,
but on the point of sleeping you turn
modest, it seems, your back towards me

and in that moment leave me feeling
- not solitary, exactly, but ... unconsoled.
I have my strategies: catch you, once you've fallen,

in an embrace you don't reciprocate, and breathe
your vanilla breath, an essence I now know
as well as this spine which comes between us

embodying what can never be said; self-evident
as a warm fossil embedded in the sheets;
or a history in Braille - syllables of bone

legible only because you trust me enough
to turn your back on me, turning alone
into the unintelligible night, to sleep.

*Gregory Warren Wilson*

# Frantically splashing in Lacoste

Without them the pool is a lonely place,
The two who are not with me,
No more shout; spray and laugh
Have abandoned me.

Until floating on my back
I can make them out behind the far up window.
I wave and my wife steps sideways out of sight,
No answering wave from her,

Leaving our small daughter standing quite still on the ledge
Looking down, looking down, looking down,
On the old man who is now splashing so frantically for her
attention
The father who is not yet old to her.

In later life will this be her first memory of me
And my last memory of her?

*Michael Young*

# Upside Down

I weigh plus and minus
from my window bay of this room:
wait, in a wide glance of sky,
stark verdict on the evens test
I can't affect; the 50:50 chance
to fail (or pass) without a try.
The only sway I owned -
whether or not to know.

Under the blown silk curve
of belling sky, this wash of blue,
recollect a day I didn't mean to know.
How, across a surgery's reception hatch,
I picked from scattered index cards
urgent words inked in red:
HIV+ - to come in
and walked home wondering who.

No surprise in this: thin men there
were passing tapestry with gulls, pier lights,
distant ships; temporary beneath the high stretch
of sea to sky, that wide blue fix.
What bothered me was casually knowing it:
that a phone would ring; disturb the stillness
of his morning bath - the suds bursting and crackling
around forgotten amber, the soap dissolving.

And wonder now where my card waits –
whether, momentarily, it will attract the eye
of receptionist, passing visitor to the ward;
if someone will decipher, across a shoulder,
from wrong side of a desk:  Carcinoma
- that casual knowing while I still lie in either/or;
this calm before my world
could turn itself upside down.

*Elizabeth Barrett*

'

# The inexpensive present

You know the crackle ice-cubes make,
Plunged from the freezer into juice,

And the fizzing song of hot fruit-cake
As the blade comes clean from its heart,

And how day-old snow surrenders to a shoe
With the underwater creak of shampooed hair,

And how balsam seedpods, when they're ripe,
Burst if you finger them lightly like this?

*Felicity Wyvern*

# Song

It is so easy being lazy, lying on
my flat back under the free shades of
nyme trees.
One rises from dozing on daily gifts
of sunlight, rain clouds, harmattan chills or dust,
served on long tropical days.
When a burst of ambition flaps my
wings I am told Big Eye has a show
which has been running before the sun caught fire
and I am a mere detail in it.
With my soul thus emptied of pride and purpose,
It is difficult shouting *I am*.

*Okello Oculi*

# The changing debate in Scotland

## Devolution, home rule and self-government

### Gerry Hassan

*Gerry Hassan explores Scottishness and Britishness in the new Scotland.*

Scotland has finally established its Parliament - after more than one hundred years of debate on devolution and home rule, thirty-plus Bills presented to the Commons, two referendums and two Scotland Acts receiving Royal Assent. This is an historic event, especially since, prior to 1 May 1997, many observers thought that the British road to devolution, rather like the British road to socialism, was an impossible path open only to idealists, revolutionaries and cranks.

The term 'home rule' has been used in debates about a Scottish Parliament for over one hundred years - it was first used in relation to Scotland by Gladstone in 1879; while 'devolution' became more prominent from the 1970s onwards. Despite being used interchangeably, they have very different meanings - devolution emphasising power retained with the UK Parliament and British sovereignty, and home rule being a more radical form of decentralisation and Scottish popular sovereignty. It was no accident that in debates in the 1980s, the term 'home rule' made a comeback, to denote a break with the devolution proposals of the 1970s.

Debates about a Scottish Parliament have been interwoven with the demand for Scottish self-government, but the latter is a wider political term than any constitutional reform. Supporters of a Parliament have tended to assume that it will automatically lead to greater democratisation of Scottish life, but in fact this can only happen via the active will and choice of the Scottish people.

This article will focus on a number of key long-term issues about Scottish politics and its place in the Union, addressing the characteristics of Scottish nationalism, and the interplay between Scottish unionisms and nationalisms. The prospects for engaging with multiple, as opposed to exclusive, identities will be analysed, and this will include the championing of a progressive Scottish-British identity. The post-devolution environment of Scotland will be assessed, looking at domestic politics north of the border, and also at its involvement in UK debates. Finally, the future of Scottish politics will be assessed, looking from the first Scottish Parliamentary elections onwards.

## What is contemporary Scottish nationalism?

Modern day Scottish nationalism should not be confused either with the SNP or with earlier Scottish national identities preserved in the Treaty of Union. The Union with England in 1707 preserved the 'holy trinity' of institutional autonomy - the Church, law and education - which were seen as defending Scottish distinctiveness and nationhood; but contemporary Scottish nationalism owes its existence to broader and looser socio-economic and cultural factors. Equally, though, Scottish nationalism cannot be equated with the rise of the SNP, for the two have a complex and changing relationship.

Contemporary Scottish nationalism shot to prominence with the victory of the SNP in the 1967 Hamilton by-election: a victory which coincided with the crisis of British social democracy as the Wilson Government prevaricated over devaluation and abandoned its National Plan. In the 1970s, the SNP's support reached a peak as the post-war consensus fell apart and the Labour government was thrown from crisis to crisis, and tried to hold the line in Scotland by the expedient of introducing devolution proposals it had not thought through or believed in.

In the 1960s and 1970s, the SNP's surge ignited Scottish politics and Scottish nationalism, but after the twin debacle of 1979, when the devolution referendum proved inconclusive, and the Tories were returned, SNP support waned; however, at this time Scottish nationalism reinvented itself as a broad cultural and political movement not located in any one party. During the height of the Thatcher years, the opposition to the Tories was characterised by the national dimension, and the coming together of a centre-left and Scottish national agenda which included Labour and the SNP.

Many on the centre-left in Scotland and the UK still have a problem with Scottish nationalism, seeing the dark, evil forces of nationalism as responsible for much that has been wrong in the world from Nazi Germany to the disintegration of Yugoslavia. However, to understand the forces of Scottish nationalism we need to locate it in a very different tradition of nationalism which has been called neo-nationalism. The analysis by David McCrone of neo-nationalism can be summed up as follows:

◆ Neo-nationalism occurs in coherent civil societies which are not independent states, but have a degree of political autonomy.
◆ There is a complex relationship between cultural and political nationalism which emphasises 'civic' rather than 'ethnic' nationalism.
◆ Multiple national identities, rather than mono-cultural identities are the norm: Scots and British, Catalans and Spanish, Quebecois and Canadian.
◆ The self-government movement is not aligned with support for one party - the nationalist movement is defined as bigger than the major nationalist party.
◆ There is an ambiguity about the aims of the nationalist party and whether it supports full-scale independence, seen in phrases such as 'home rule', 'autonomisme', 'Souverainete-Association' or 'Consociation'.
◆ A variable geometry of power exists, with political debates taking place on three levels: the nation, the state and supra-state such as the European Union.[1]

Mainstream Scottish nationalism matches these and other criteria. It addresses both vertical and horizontal processes and identities placing itself within the tradition of neo or post-nationalism. Some of those on the left who seek to deny this, such as Eric Hobsbawm, come from a Marxist tradition which

---

1.  David McCrone, *The Sociology of Nationalism: Tomorrow's Ancestors*, Routledge 1998, pp. 128-29.

attempted to differentiate the diverse traditions of socialisms and communisms, but somehow baulks at attempting a similar process with nationalism.[2] In Hobsbawm's worldview, Serbian, Palestinian, Scottish and Catalan nationalism all contain within them the seeds of an ethnic, exclusive, politics which could lead to a reactionary agenda.

## Scottish unionisms and nationalisms

The forces of Scottish unionisms and nationalisms have been in a dynamic discourse where they influence and interact with each other. Unionism is a narrative which prioritises the importance of British identity in Scotland and the centrality of the Union with England; Scottish nationalism as a phenomena has stressed the importance of Scottish identity, culture and history. Both perspectives have complex and ever-changing relationships with each other and the issue of a Scottish Parliament, but both have tended to define themselves as 'Scottish' and acknowledge and wish to preserve the degree of Scottish distinctiveness that exists within the Union.

Scottish unionism and nationalism have changed themselves, what they represent and their agendas many times in post-war Scottish politics. Scottish unionism's decline during the Tory years saw it associated with the uncompromising English nationalism of Thatcherism, but this concealed the rich diversity of unionism and its continued majority support. Scottish Labour and Liberal Democrats have always been unionist parties, but during the 1980s they chose to emphasise their Scottish nationalist credentials to differentiate themselves from the unionist Tories.

What actually differentiates Scottish unionism and nationalism is often more matters of style, language and values, rather than substance - with a substantial degree of overlap between the two. A useful way of understanding contemporary Scottish politics is to imagine Scottish unionism and nationalism as two large circles which intersect and overlap each other more than they are separate entities. This defines the terrain of modern Scottish politics and identity with three areas: a unionism of exclusive British identity; a unionist-Scottish nationalism of Scots and British identities - John P.

---

2. Eric Hobsbawm, *Nations and Nationalism since 1780: Programme, Myth and Reality*, Cambridge University Press 1990.

Mackintosh's famous 'dual identity'; and a Scottish nationalism of exclusive Scottish identity. The balance between these three areas has shifted dramatically in post-war times, with the first declining and the third expanding: an exclusive unionism now represents about one in ten Scots, the middle ground - 'dual identities' - over 50 per cent, while exclusive Scottishness totals about one-third of Scots.[3]

A number of factors can be read into these figures. There has been a significant shift away from Britishness and towards Scottishness, but it is also true that the majority of Scots reject exclusive identities as Scots or British, and see no contradiction between embracing both Scottishness and Britishness. And while one way of looking at the figures is to add the Scots-British 'dual identities' to exclusive Scots to get figures of 70-80 per cent with a Scots identity, one can just as easily add the Scots-British 'dual identities' to exclusive Britishness to get approximately 60 per cent who see themselves as British.

However, what happened during Thatcherism was that a caricature of unionism became common currency in Scottish politics. Unionists became defined as anti-home rule and even anti-Scottish, whereas nationalists were seen as pro-home rule and pro-Scottish. This simplistic dichotomy does an injustice to the rich traditions in both these perspectives, and hides the basic truth that a majority of unionists have always in recent years been pro-home rule, and only a minority of even the unionist persuasion have opposed a Scottish Parliament.

The emergent politics of Scottish nationalism which have defined and reshaped much of Scottish politics in the last twenty years contains many disparate and diverse trends. The dominant strand of Scottish nationalism as discussed earlier is the neo-nationalist, civic, inclusive, cosmopolitan politics looking outwards to Western Europe and its successful small nations: Ireland, Norway and Sweden. This strand is championed by the SNP leadership and a majority of the party, but would also include most of the Labour and Liberal Democrats and large elements of Scottish civil society.

Another strand of Scots nationalism which has been enjoying a new

---

3.   Alice Brown, David McCrone, Lindsay Paterson, and Paula Surridge, *The Scottish Electorate: The 1997 General Election and Beyond*, Macmillan 1999, Ch. 6.

sense of strength in the last few years is the unreflective, unthinking, romanticising politics of *Braveheart* - 'Rise Now and Be a Nation Again' - which was appropriated by the Scottish *Sun*. The *Daily Record* ran a 'I am a Real Scot' campaign which included bylines such as 'I am a Real Scot from Bathgate' - emphasising dubious notions of authenticity as well as a sense of place and residence.

This outlook can often be combined with a completely apolitical outlook on the world, which has taken hold across diverse groups in Scotland, from the middle-class rugby fans of Murrayfield to working-class estates - they celebrate all things Scottish uncritically and pose English identity as 'an other'. Some of this perspective can be found in SNP grassroots members, but because of its apoliticalness it can also be found in Labour and even Tory voters.

The third segment of Scots nationalism significantly overlaps with the second, and has a profoundly atavistic, ethnic-based sense of identity, championing an exclusive sense of Scottishness, and wary of a pluralist, multicultural and multiracial Scotland, and in particular English 'white settlers'. Rooted in such micro-groups as Settler Watch, the numbers who subscribe to such a narrow, blinkered view are minuscule, but its influence creeps into wider elements of Scottish society.

These three strands of Scots nationalism are not meant as an exclusive list of the elements that make up a contradictory and pluralist creed, but they give an idea of its diversity. Different groups react to the umbrella term 'Scottish nationalism' in different ways: the pre-1979 centre-left for example still tends in many places to worry about the darker side of nationalism and to equate it with fascism, racism and other xenophobic forces; whereas the post-1979 Scottish left have reclaimed nationalism as their own, and intertwined the politics of self-government and solidarity. The differences between these two groups can often be found running through Labour CLPs, trade unions and civil society.

## The British dimension to Scotland

In the 1980s the British state and Britishness became identified in Scotland with the political project of Thatcherism. A Scottish/British discourse grew which emphasised the positive aspects of Scottish identity: centre-left, social democratic, community-minded - while Britishness was perceived as right-wing, racist, individualistic and Thatcherite.

These assumptions are questionable from both sides of the border. From a Scottish point of view, they reinforced a number of 'myths' about Scottish difference - over-emphasising and sentimentalising Scottish difference, while writing off Britain as right-wing and England as lost forever to the Tories. This misread English politics and the limited appeal of Thatcherism.

A number of consequences follow on from the rise of this Scottish/British faultline. First, this stereotyping did allow a wide array of Scots to feel more self-confident about their identity by posing a virtuous, if ideal, type of Scottishness. Second, this politics of myths reinforced the conservative agenda of the Scottish centre-left, preoccupied as

> 'Britishness was perceived as right-wing, racist, individualistic and Thatcherite'

it has been with old industries, work and the politics of decline. Third, the dismissal of British identity problematicised it at a Scottish level, so that the articulation of British identities and British nationalisms in Scotland became more difficult.

A majority of Scots have always identified with a sense of both Scottishness and Britishness; they have not seen any contradiction between the two, and have continued to reject the exclusive identity politics of either British or Scottish nationalism. One of the crucial areas for the future of Scottish politics, and particularly for Scottish Labour, will be how successfully it can address a politics that is both Scottish and British at the same time, and develop a new kind of inclusive politics around which support for the home rule settlement can be anchored.

The advocates of an exclusive politics have come from some likely and unlikely quarters. The SNP and the broader nationalist movement have had an obvious interest in talking up the Scottishing of Scottish politics; but other groups have played an equally important part. Academics and the media have been able to increase their influence and status by writing of the distinctiveness of Scotland, rather than its similarities with the rest of the UK. In response to this, a part of the centre-left, wedded to an anti-nationalist politics, has taken refuge in a British agenda which sees Scot Nats behind everything that goes wrong in Scotland.

All of this causes potential problems for those wishing to redefine a Scottish-

British agenda for the new Scotland. For Scottish Labour, the leading party of Scotland for the last forty years, this is acutely so. During the 1980s, Labour put itself at the head of the broad nationalist movement in Scotland by its signing of *A Claim of Right* and its involvement in the cross-party Scottish Constitutional Convention. This meant that the Scottish party became increasingly defined as nationalist, while it placed less stress on its British credentials. This began to prove troublesome with the advent of Blair and New Labour, who forcibly reintroduced a British perspective with the announcement of the two question referendum on a Scottish Parliament in 1996.

Scottish Labour has behaved in a rudderless and disorientated fashion since the arrival of Blair. This is partly because of limitations in the Blair British orientated strategy - which aided the establishment of a Parliament via a referendum - which does not understand the complexities of Scottish politics. However, it is also due to the deficiencies in the Scottish based agenda of Labour politicians, which is in favour of a return to Labour's successful 1980s Scottish nationalist strategy, which centred on traditional values and an oppositionalist mentality.

Any new political strategy by Scottish Labour, Liberal Democrats and Conservatives - the mainstream British parties - has to develop on two different levels and agendas. They need to develop policies and politics for the Scottish and British Parliaments, and develop an agenda for Scotland which draws on the traditions of unionism and nationalism: Scottish and British identities. In drawing on these traditions, some of the old-fashioned identities may prove more troublesome than helpful, but by trying to build a new hybrid, pluralist politics for a new political settlement we can invent new traditions and language.

## Scotland after the Act: Scottish domestic politics

Scottish politics post-devolution will be driven in ways which will make them very different from politics up until now. With a new, broadly proportional, electoral system for the Scottish Parliament, and a seemingly long-term realignment of Scottish politics taking place, we are now entering uncharted waters.

The Scottish Parliament's electoral system means that the parliament will always broadly represent the balance of support for Scotland's four main political parties. It will reflect that they are all minorities and should develop policies and practices which reflect this. This fundamental change is being aided by the transformation of Scottish politics - which began even before the Parliament sat, with the Labour Party's long established dominance being challenged by a newly resurgent SNP. This may reflect the beginning of a realignment of politics, with Scotland slowly moving away from an asymmetrical system of one party dominance, to a two party competitive system between Labour and SNP. This sea-change is only occurring at the Scottish Parliament elections, with Labour's Westminster dominance continuing relatively unchallenged. This experience of multi-layered democracy - of the nationalist party doing better at the autonomous level than at the nation-state level - is similar to the politics of Catalunya.

These changes will require a new kind of politics from across the political spectrum which will take time to emerge. The first elections have seen some signs of this and some resistance. Both the Labour Party and SNP have fought the elections in the old-fashioned adversarial Westminster style of winner-takes-all, implying that victory gives them the mythical mantra of 'mandate'. This reflects the struggle for ascendancy between them: their battle for the ragged soul of centre-left Scottish social democracy, their similarities, and thus, their need for differentiation.

A different set of pressures has influenced the Liberal Democrats and the Conservatives. Both parties have been marginalised in terms of support by the titanic and often ugly battle between Labour and SNP, and have been reduced in electoral terms in the medium and long-term. The Conservatives once gained over half the Scottish vote in 1955, but have been in inexorable decline since, gaining 31 per cent at the start of the Thatcher era in 1979, 17.5 per cent in 1997 and 15 per cent in the first Scottish Parliament elections second vote. The Liberal Democrats, as the Alliance, won 24 per cent in 1983, falling back at each election, to 13 per cent in 1997 and 1999.

Both parties have reacted to the politics of decline by using the possibilities of the new electoral system to offer different options in which they would be prepared to be part of a governing coalition. In the Conservatives' case, this has seen them offer the implausible scenario of working with Labour to save the Union; but the it has allowed the Lib Dems to develop their key role as the anchor and future kingmaker party of Scottish politics, even with such a minimal base. The Lib Dems will probably decide in future elections whether Labour or SNP forms an administration. In the meantime Labour has been dragging its feet, showing the arrogance of old-style politics, insisting that its preferred option is a minority, rather than coalition government supported by the Lib Dems. They, to their credit, have insisted on a coalition government and an agreed programme.

The long-term implications of the Scottish Parliament and the above factors are that Labour's one-party dominance is coming to an end, not just at a national, but regional and local level. The politics of Labour one-party areas like the West of Scotland and Glasgow, where Labour politics have run into problems associated with machine politics - corruption, cronyism, malpractice and incompetence - will be slowly changed. A new age is coming to local government, which will be transformed by proportional representation, smaller councils, elected Provosts, and executive government, to produce a more open, pluralist system which will be easier to scrutinise and more relevant to the modern age of government by citizens.

What difference will all this political and institutional change make to Scottish polity? What different policy models might emerge in Scotland post-devolution which aid innovation and radicalism rather than the conservatism of the Scottish political establishment? The campaign for a Scottish Parliament in the last twenty years has been sadly dominated, to the point of exclusion, with achieving a Parliament and perfecting the institutional and political structures around it; little to no thought has been given to the policy agenda, ideas and vision that the Parliament should be tapping into, and this comes from the complacency of the centre-left consensus, which has automatically assumed that because the Parliament will be its creation it will automatically be a radical body.

Two fundamentally different realities are at odds here. The conservatism of the Scottish political establishment and Scottish political culture has been strengthened; it sees itself as vindicated by its opposition to Thatcherism and the establishment of the Parliament. The dominant strand of the Scottish centre-left, found across Labour, SNP, the STUC and large parts of civil society, sees a Scottish Parliament as a signal that Scottish society was right to resist the radical change of Thatcherism (which it was), but, following on from that, they also believe that the Scottish internal status quo which they were defending - the pre-1979 Scotland of order and certainty - can be maintained in a slightly rearranged fashion. This is the politics of labourist Scotland: a right-wing administrative politics of institutionalised dominance, which has distorted and limited democracy and innovation.

However, the Scottish people have different expectations. While the Scottish political elite sees the Parliament as a green light for a managed and ordered politics, the public have very different priorities and expect the Parliament to introduce widespread and positive change across a range of areas of life. From education, health and housing to social policy, where the Parliament has responsibility, Scots voters by sizeable majorities expect change; but they also expect it in areas where the Parliament does not have responsibility - the economy and redistribution.[4] This shows that, as is often the case, the public are ahead of the politicians in the debate - and if the newly elected 129 MSPs think they can spend their first years bedding down the Parliament and successfully completing their induction courses on joined-up thinking and holistic government, they are in for a surprise.

The Parliament only has a narrow window of opportunity. At the moment, it is not seen by the public as being about 'politics' and 'politicians', but is instead seen as belonging to the Scottish people. This will not remain the case for long, once the institution gets up and running, and the new political class starts acting as an emerging elite which narrows debate and openness; so in its first six months to one year the Parliament has to introduce some significant and symbolic policies and processes which show that it intends to be a different kind of institution.

## Scotland after the Act: the United Kingdom dimension

Scotland's relations with the UK Parliament can be shaped by a willingness to compromise and forge a new partnership on both sides and to accept creative tension and conflict as inherent in the settlement. A number of different scenarios are possible in relations between the Scottish Parliament and Westminster which are illustrated overleaf:

---

4. *The Scottish Electorate, op. cit.*

| Scottish Parliament: | Westminster Parliament: |
|---|---|

HARMONY
Acts within remit

Does not interfere in Scottish affairs

UK LED CONFLICT
Acts within remit

Interferes in Scottish affairs

SCOTTISH LED CONFLICT
Acts beyond remit

Does not interfere in Scottish affairs

MAXIMUM CONFLICT
Acts beyond remit

Interferes in Scottish affairs

In the first years of the Parliament, with a Labour Government in Westminster and Labour-Liberal Democrat coalition in Scotland, the likelihood is that all sides will try to make the new settlement and institutions work as harmoniously as possible. However, in the medium to longer-term, conflict is bound to arise, particularly when different political parties end up in government in Westminster and Scotland, and the new arrangements are most tested.

Disagreement and conflict could be from either side with the UK Parliament acting beyond its remit by legislating in a devolved area or taking up an issue like the Barnett Formula or the West Lothian Question and single-handedly changing the arrangements in a way detrimental to the Scottish Parliament. On the other hand, the Scots Parliament, particularly, if led by an SNP administration, could attempt to legislate on a reserved matter to Westminster such as defence policy and the Trident nuclear submarines in the Clyde.

It is even possible if we had the SNP running Scotland, and a right-wing Conservative Government in London, that both sides could exceed their agreed remits, and in such instability Scottish independence would become more likely. The challenge to the new institutions over the forthcoming period, will be to channel the conflict and tensions that are bound to exist and be raised in positive ways, so that decisions which were once taken within the Whitehall Civil Service about public spending, become the preserve of a wider policy community and general public.

A key element in the new evolving character of the United Kingdom is the Blair Government's radical, but in some ways limited, programme of constitutional reform. The Labour Government has unleashed a welter of constitutional change since May 1997: with a Scottish Parliament, Welsh and Northern Irish Assemblies, a Greater London Authority and Mayor, PR for the European elections, and incorporation of the European Convention on Human Rights.

However, this welter of change has obscured that most of these proposals were changes Blair inherited from the Kinnock and Smith years. In different respects, these were either qualified tactically, as in referenda for the Scottish Parliament and Welsh Assembly, and the self-denying ordinance imposed on Scottish Labour on the Parliament's tax raising powers. More fundamental retreats were undertaken on Labour's commitment to English regionalism, which have now been left with Regional Development Agencies and a fudged, confused policy of indirectly elected regional chambers leading to assemblies where there is demand, amounting to a recipe for inaction.

What these retreats and manoeuvres have illustrated is Labour's confusion over constitutional reform and the lack of a 'big picture', vision or sense of destination. The Labour Government, like most UK governments, does not really understand the character of the UK in terms of nations, identities and cultures, as all the glossy talk about 'Cool Britannia' and 'the new Britain' shows. They have exemplified a schizophrenic attitude to the changing British constitution: sometimes pretending nothing has changed and the old order is intact, and at others invoking constitutional reform to prove its radical credentials. Both the Scottish Parliament and Human Rights Bill White Paper went out of their ways to emphasis that Westminster remained the supreme Parliament in these isles and the continuation of the absolute doctrine of parliamentary sovereignty; this is an attitude we have seen before with UK Governments in relation to the process of European integration from 1972 onward and is not one that should fill us with optimism.

This Government sees the UK as a unitary state with one central locus of power and sovereignty dispensing out various forms of intermediate government, whereas in reality, the UK has never been a unitary state. How could a state with the distinct arrangements that were agreed and preserved to Scotland in the Treaty of Union, ever be perceived of as a unitary state except by the most misinformed elements of the English political classes? Tam Dalyell, that sad ghost of the 1970s devolution debates, was actually right when he argued then that devolution was not possible in a unitary state, but devolution is possible, in a state like the UK that is not a unitary, but a union state.[5]

A union state allows for different local and regional arrangements and degrees of decentralism, and importantly, the preserving of pre-union rights, which is how the Treaty of Union should be seen. The politics of a union state, are positioned in-between those of a unitary state and the Franco-German idea of federalism which has driven forward ideas of European integration and allows for an asymmetrical programme of devolution, and the development of a rolling programme of English regional reform which will take time to evolve, but which will allow different patchwork solutions as outcomes, with a quasi-federal settlement as one endpoint. And such a flexible politics of 'variable geometry' would match the political needs of the European Union and allow the UK to influence this, as much as draw from it, developing a more citizen based EU than the Franco-German corporatist model.

## The future of Scottish politics

The first Scottish Parliamentary elections in May 1999 were the most fundamental test yet of the Labour government, and the new constitutional settlement that is emerging. While Labour won 39 per cent of the first vote to the SNP's 29 per cent, Scottish Labour's second vote fell to 34 per cent - its lowest since the debacle of 1931 - while the SNP won 27 per cent. This has resulted in Labour winning 56 seats, the SNP 35, Conservatives 18, Liberal Democrats 17 and others 3. This means that Labour, with 34 per cent of second votes, received 44 per cent of seats - a result not that proportional, but a vast improvement on the distortions of FPTP.

Some longer-term implications can be taken from the first elections. First, the Scottish elections will tend to be interpreted outside Scotland in relation to the SNP vote. A high SNP vote, producing a close-run election for Labour,

---

5.  Stein Rokkan, and Derek Urwin, Introduction, in *The Politics of Territorial Identity: Studies in European Regionalism*, Sage 1982.

would have been equated south of the border with an imminent crisis of the Union and the inevitable break-up of the UK. This kind of simplistic scenario is all the British press are capable of understanding about Scottish politics, because their interest in the subject is intermittent and usually contained to periods of SNP popularity.

The relatively low SNP vote (30 per cent or under was regarded by most commentators as low) has to be seen against the unrealistic expectations the SNP raised last year when it briefly took the lead in polls against Labour. Such an SNP performance has to be seen in the context of the transitional character of the first Scottish Parliament elections. These elections are the first results in an emerging process of politics in a multi-layered democracy, where there can be a substantial difference in voting intentions between the Scottish Parliament and Westminster elections; the end of Labour one-party dominance in Scotland, was always going to be a slow, gradual change, rather than a big bang. The SNP vote of 29 per cent in the first vote is historically a good result; but it will be interpreted south of the border as a triumphant vindication of Scottish Labour and the defeat of Scottish nationalism. However, what it does reveal as an unpalatable truth for the SNP is the strength and salience of British identities and nationalisms beyond such short-term factors as NATO's bombing of Kosovo.

Scottish politics work in a dynamic which is slightly different from that which the British press understands. Scottish voters have used the SNP for the last thirty years to cajole, annoy and signal to Westminster and the other Scottish political parties that they wanted change, that they didn't want to be taken for granted, or that they wanted extra monies from the Treasury. All of Scotland's other political parties, Labour, Conservatives and Lib Dems, have used the threat of the SNP to win more clout for Scotland: Thomas Johnston, Labour's Scottish Secretary in the Churchill Coalition Government during the war, used to talk up the Nationalist threat to Churchill at a time when it was near to non-existent, and Willie Ross, Wilson's Secretary of State, and so-called 'hammer of the Nats', used the nationalists' popularity in the 1960s to win more public spending for Scotland. The new Scottish Parliament merely institutionalises and formalises these processes - which can be caricatured as pork-barrel politics, but are inevitable in multi-layered democracies.

In the next five to ten years, Scottish politics will settle down to making the new settlement work, and deciding on the issue of formal independence or not.

A new politics, which is not about one-party rule, will develop, which will require all the actors to develop new attitudes. This will bring centre stage the strengths, divisions and attitudes of the non-Labour Scotland majority, which will coalesce increasingly around the SNP - which will at some point after the first elections form a Scottish administration. This will be a defining point for the emergence of a new, pluralist kind of Scottish politics, very different from the old labourist order; for Labour, despite never having won a majority of the Scottish vote, has seen itself as a hegemonic party in Scotland, and has never understood the hopes and fears of non-Labour Scotland; and in particular, they have failed to understand the fear shared by many, of being governed by the old Labour one-party state.

The first Scottish administration - a Labour-Liberal Democrat formal coalition with an agreed four year programme - is a vital first step in the transition from the old to the new; it allows Labour to recognise that it is a minority, not majority, party, and, through co-operating with the Lib Dems, will allow them to govern as part of a majority alliance, with inputs into the non-Labour majority in Scotland. In the longer-term, an SNP-led administration is an inevitability in Scotland, as is a referendum on Scotland's constitutional status in the UK - which from today's vantage point would be a close-run result.

The future of Scotland is still an open book. Although some see 'independence' as inevitable in the next ten years, we need to be clear that, while at the moment most Scots do not fear independence, nor have they made their minds up. or reached a clear understanding about, what the relative terms 'devolution' and 'independence' actually mean in an interdependent world. As for Tom Nairn's argument that Britishness is somehow in terminal decline, if this is true at a UK level, it is showing a remarkably vibrant health across a number of areas, and is still capable of attracting majority support amongst Scots.[6] Nothing is inevitable or decided about the future of Scotland beyond that it is in the hands of Scottish people to make the modern nation and society they want.

The SNP leadership has a post-nationalist vision, aiming to position the SNP in the tradition of the Convergencia i Unio, rather than Parti Quebecois, of autonomy rather than separatism. This transformation of the SNP was

6. Tom Nairn, *After Britain*, Granta 1999.

happening before our very eyes in the first Scottish elections, but the Labour Party does not want to let go of the old Nat stereotypes - of tartan Tories, of independence equalling separatism, and of an ethnic, narrow politics leading to the divorce of the UK. At some point, perhaps - after the SNP have won a Scottish election, are successfully running a devolved Scotland and are continuing to do so after an independence referendum has been narrowly lost - Labour will eventually wake up to the realities of the new Scotland: that the SNP and Labour share the same heritage and agendas, of trying to reinvent and modernise Scottish social democracy, and that the SNP's rise and challenging of the discredited old Labour order has been a defining point in Scottish politics, in the best long-term interests of Scotland, and Labour as well.

# Cultural fishing

## Jo Littler

Christopher H. J. Bradley, *Mrs Thatcher's Cultural Policies: 1979 - 1990: A comparative study of the globalized cultural system*, Columbia University Press 1998, $28

Since the mid-1980s an increasing amount of attention has been paid to cultural policy by academics, journalists, policy-makers and advisors. Geoff Mulgan and Ken Worpole's brilliant and succinct *Saturday Night or Sunday Morning?* was one early example of this attention; it acted both as a concise excavation of the history of the cultural policies offered by the left, and as a polemical manifesto urging Labour to adopt more of the culturally populist strategies of the GLC. More recently, cultural policy has become an increasingly visible as an academic field in its own right, as courses (such as at Warwick) and journals (the *International Journal of Cultural Policy*) have been established. The cultural politics and social histories shaping (and shaped by) British cultural policy have become more thoroughly interrogated (for example in Andrew Blake's and Jim McGuigan's work); and one of the main points of Tony Bennett's recent book *Culture: A Reformer's Science* was that cultural studies should be more concerned with its actual and potential relationship to policy. *Mrs Thatcher's Cultural Policies*, therefore, sounds from its title like a timely publication, one which should be a useful addition to these debates; it might, hopefully, generate greater understanding of the frameworks and constraints inherited by New Labour's Department of Culture, Media and Sport (otherwise known as DCMS, or Don't Call Me Socialist), and of the frameworks and constraints with which it continues to negotiate.

This is a long (400-page) book, which is broad in scope and has clearly involved a great deal of research. The perhaps slightly misleading subtitle refers to a comparison of British arts policy and cultural industries as entities in a globalised cultural marketplace (although there is in fact little attention paid to globalisation), rather than to a comparison of British cultural policy with that of other countries (although this is briefly mentioned). Dipping in and out of a wide array of cultural histories and industries, the chapters range from local authority funding to the music business, from the cable and satellite industry to the archaically titled 'intellectuals and the churches'. It does not draw on much existing work on cultural policy, nor does it appear to be too familiar with writing on Thatcherism or neo-liberalism. However, Andrew Gamble's work on Thatcherism is drawn on in the book's definition of the two main, conflicting arts policy priorities of the Thatcher decade: firstly, that of 'freeing the market' and reducing state spending in all areas; and secondly, the linked priorities of vigorous centralisation, consolidation of national identity, and attraction of tourist revenue.

Policies made on 'the arts' during the Thatcher years involved the erosion of state subsidy, the encouragement of private and business spending, and the refashioning of the state arts bodies in terms of corporate business practice. Dismantling the previous social democratic/liberal consensus that access to elite arts for all was every citizen's right, these policies at the same time extended a High Art discourse through - and into - wider corporate use, and compounded the undemocratic tendencies pre-existing within the state 'arts' sector. The extensive use of public money to privilege and support the private sector took place through such mechanisms as the circulation by the Office of Arts and Libraries of leaflets with titles like *The Arts are Your Business*, through the extension of such bodies as The Association for Business Sponsorship in the Arts (ABSA), and by the 1984 formation of the Business Sponsorship Incentive Scheme (BSIS).

Simultaneously, the specifically entrepreneurial populism of Thatcherite conservatism began to dismantle the hegemony of the old Establishment and freeze out the 'Great and the Good'. The previous 'gentlemanly' agreements of cross-party appointments were by and large abolished, and the arts establishment's Old Boy network (white, male upper/middle-class, privately educated), like that in other sectors, was infiltrated by a barrage of New Boys - mainly white, self-made businessmen - through (often direct) government patronage. As Bradley points out, arts policy-making institutions, specifically the Arts Council, were retained despite the imperative to dismantle state arts spending, in part because their old conservative structure remained a convenient way of fostering right-wing middlebrow culture, and a useful mechanism of political patronage.

The often labyrinthine mechanisms of arts policy-making institutions can be hard to understand, and this book is a helpful in explicating them, just as it is useful for piecing together the complex relationship between the Arts Council, various arts quangos and the policies of the Thatcher government.

Bradley continually describes the corporate transformation of the public arts sector as a search for 'more efficient administration' in which arts bodies were 'taught how to fish'. The phrase is borrowed from Richard Luce, a minister for Arts and Libraries in the 1980s, whose corporate proverb was 'Give a person a fish and you feed him for a day; teach him how to fish and you feed him for life'.

And what soon becomes clear is that, despite, or including, occasional lurches to the left, this a book for which public sector fishing for corporate sponsorship is not really a problematic issue. This is indicated at the beginning of the book when we are introduced to what are the 'two antagonistic views' about *Mrs Thatcher's Cultural Policies*:

> The common view is that she did not have one at all. At the other extreme certain left-wing critics argue the case for a carefully structured hegemonic plan in the cultural field. [...] It is clear that both views have their relative strengths and weaknesses, but the truth must logically lie somewhere in-between (p1).

This characteristic let's-not-get-too-extreme liberal stance structures the entire book; it is a kind of analysis that only understands 'hegemony' as conspiracy theory; one which continually contests the idea that Mrs Thatcher was part of the New Right, or argues that she was not 'being political' on the grounds that she was 'too pragmatic'. In this, the book quickly reveals how what it clearly constructs as its own impartial and objective common sense has been structured through Thatcherism, in a way that it would never recognise itself. This is particularly blatant in some passages:

> Another area where there was very limited action was social security. This is, likewise, a stunning example of Mrs Thatcher's pragmatism as opposed to to what her critics termed her ideological outlook. [...] The fact that the social security system was retained, although not for young people between 16 and 19, shows the extent of Mrs Thatcher's political pragmatism (pp374-5).

It is an example of the influence of both Blairite rhetoric and of its Thatcherite roots that 'pragmatism' and 'practicality' is read throughout the text as the opposite of manipulative 'ideology'. The fact that this extract is about social security is also indicative of the extent to which the term 'culture' is neither described nor discussed. This in part appears to be because it is written out of that entrenched position from and for which (High) Culture is so astoundingly obvious a category that it is taken as a given that it does not need to be described or discussed. In this vein, Bradley's discussion of opera, for example, is described in terms laden with superlatives like 'excellent' and 'first-rate', without any interrogation of the criteria through which these judgements are made. And it is in this vein at the end of the book that he belatedly begins to take Thatcher to task for apparently not producing 'a new version of culture':

> It was at a Royal Academy dinner in May 1980, when Mrs Thatcher was to say: 'We should see to it that our people are steeped in a real knowledge and understanding of our national culture'. In 1990, when she had to resign, the work still needed to be done. However, in all fairness, should a prime minister be expected to do it? Are we not asking too much of her, to lead the country and at the same time to come out with a new version of culture? The premier did not achieve all that she had promised to do, but then, should a cultural transformation be expected from any individual? (p414)

This comes right in the last paragraph, and it is the first time the rationale for appointing 'Mrs Thatcher' rather than Thatcherism as the book's point of focus is even so much as commented on. (And when it is, 'we' are all made responsible through persistently 'asking too much' of the poor lady.) The main concern and analytic focus of the book is trained on the space between what the individualised figure said and what she did (what he calls her 'implementation gap'). There are also some extremely reactionary sections in the text, the most repugnant being a chapter on the Press in which Eddie Shah is described as 'the saviour of Fleet Street', and in which the 1980s 'modernising' crushing of the unions over their 'abuse of power' is positively celebrated (p172).

Okay, so this book clearly offers a liberal/conservative account. Given this, it is interesting to note that there is at times an unusually wide definition of 'culture' implicit in the book - as the range of the 28 chapter subjects indicates - which runs in partial conflict with the frequently narrow, traditionally elitist use. And a toe is dipped into specifically populist waters in a chapter titled 'The Nature of Popular Culture', as Bradley takes on some of these new-fangled theories that occupy the cultural studies shelves in bookshops. His version of youth culture does occur in a bizarre parallel universe in which skinheads regularly listen to Status Quo and MTV shows things called 'video clips'; and the phrase '*Common Culture*' is used in the same way as Alan Bennett might use it to imitate his aunt, rather than as a term describing a socialist utopia/lost form of cultural community. But many of the passages which starkly recount work on popular culture are approving, and they do read as if they are perhaps productive encounters for the writer. Here, though, unsurprisingly, it is ideas about the creative capabilities of the consumer/citizen that are seized on most eagerly - the model (often mythical and certainly exaggerated, but with a definite presence here) of cultural consumption as emancipatory practice, as holistic strategy of resistance and solely creative pursuit, a model which can be, as is now frequently pointed out in cultural studies texts, entirely compatible with laissez-faire economics.

One thing the book does engender is increased awareness of how, during the mid-1980s, *research* into arts institutions and cultural industries intersected with the politics of Thatcherism. Bradley points out how research on cultural policy, particularly by the Policy Studies Institute, made clear the extent to which 'the arts' were able to foster certain ideas of national identity and to attract tourist revenue. Having a barrage of statistics available, he argues, 'completely transformed the public/private debate' over arts funding, and as a result of this 'pioneering research on cultural spending' a shift was generated in Thatcherite thinking. From having considered the arts as the most extraneous aspect of government policy, after the mid-1980s the successive Thatcher governments 'dropped their doctrinaire talk of the early years', and became excited about its corporate benefits and potential compatibility with tourism (pp109-110).

Whilst this relationship was not quite so unilinear - Thatcherism also *generated* such policy analysis - it is an interesting issue to focus on. It raises the related issue of the type of policy advice which the Department of Culture, Media and Sport is both listening to and generating; and the question of the extent to which it continues or breaks with Thatcherite policies. So far the behaviour of the DCMS has been mixed. On the one hand, there have been the democratic initiatives: the significant abolition of the word 'heritage' from the Department, with all the reactionary and racist connotations it accrued; the continual interrogation of the elitist structure of the Arts Council; and the curtailing of some of the funding for the grossly over-subsidised and aesthetically elitist world of opera. On the other, there has been the early love affair with those key figures of the designer decade, Saatchi and Conran, and their aesthetic offspring, the Young British Artists; and the frequently uncritical promotion of the creative industries, in terms that are far less about popular democracy than about targeting economic export potential. There is a vast opportunity here for the creative economy to be more creative, to become more dynamically fashioned, so that it actively promotes popular democratic forms rather than pursuing the cultural dregs of Thatcherism; it is not clear yet whether DCMS will fully avail itself of this opportunity.

# Living in counter-culture

## Mike Waite

Penny Rimbaud aka J. J. Ratter, *Shibboleth - my revolting life*, AK Press, £6.95

Penny Rimbaud was the instigator and drummer of the remarkable, noisy and influential anarchist band Crass, and it is this role that AK Press have highlighted in their publicity for his autobiography. Crass's hard-edged commitment to the values and principles of punk mean that an account of Rimbaud's life in the music scene would have been of interest in itself.

But *Shibboleth* provides more. Rimbaud's achievement is to locate his career in Crass into a wider set of accounts. The book isn't neatly constructed - it jumps between different tones and styles: thoughtful, reflective autobiography, fiction, anarchist political tract, and breathless accounts of life at the core of both the hippy and punk movements. But even through the broken up narratives, where what happened in 1977 comes before what happened in 1965, a clear and interesting story is told, in which we get a real sense of the author's views, emotions and character, with his engaging sense of humour and his frankly confessed weaknesses.

Glimpses of an uneasy, distant relationship with his father shape accounts of a middle-class childhood in the 1940s and 1950s, in which early sexual experiences and the dawn of rock and roll provided the motivation and language for the young Jeremy Ratter to adopt a rebellious, bohemian stance. He insisted on going to art school, against his father's wishes, and in his early twenties was teaching art and setting up home in the run-down farm building in rural Essex which became an important base for much late 1960s/early 1970s hippy activity around London, and later spawned Crass.

The precise variables that led to Ratter playing a central role in English counter-cultural activity aren't well detailed in the book. Accounts of personal rebellion in the context of the expansion of higher education and the development of youth movements are suggestive of how his trajectory was typical of many thousands of others in the mid-late sixties. Readers who spent time in communes, at free festivals and at 'happenings' will enjoy the relevant passages here. Ratter, though, made distinctive contributions to the scene through his energy and his shaping a life around the values he'd come to adopt.

A number of personal relationships were hugely important to Ratter at this time, and his exploration of these, and his sensitive, emotional reminiscences of love and hurt are amongst the best parts of *Shibboleth*. Regret shapes reflections on careless affairs: 'with its message of "free love", the sexual revolution devastated many a relationship that might otherwise have blossomed into something far deeper than mere carnal satisfaction ... we *were* jealous, but we disguised it with intellectual rhetoric'.

Other relationships involved more emotional investment. Ratter's friendship with Phil Russell receives the detailed account it deserves: it was brief, with a tragic end, but has clearly shaped Ratter deeply, and inspired continuing commitment to the values he shared with Phil. In the early 1970s, as 'Wally Hope', Russell was the key inspiring figure amongst the 'Wallies' who established the Stonehenge free festival, showed up regularly at Windsor, and gave life to much of the counter-culture. He was the 'fast talking leader' of the 'eight Wallies of Wiltshire' who were tried for trespass under their ludicrous false names in London's High Courts in 1974. The following year, following arrest for possessing a small amount of LSD, Wally Hope was destroyed in the mental health system, 'sectioned' for alleged schizophrenia, and provided with massive doses of drugs like Largactil. Ratter's loyal campaign to prove that the authorities were to blame for Wally Hope's death has been important to him ever since.

And his anger at those authorities is one of the ingredients which led to the 'peace and love' values of '67 expressing themselves in a way which had little to do with flower-power when Crass hit the stage in 1977. Connections between the hippy movement and punk, flowing through to the more recent wave of 'DIY' radicalism, have been explored in a couple of recent books - George McKay's *Senseless Acts of Beauty* and C. J. Stone's *Fierce Dancing*. Both cite some of Rimbaud's earlier writings and draw on interviews to illustrate those continuities in values and outlook between the 1960s and 1970s which he embodies, but which could easily escape observers superficially comparing style.

It's good that Rimbaud decided to collect together some of those scattered writings and bring them together in his own account. *Shibboleth* shows much that is distinctive in Rimbaud's journey - as an individual, he's atypical in personally being involved in two big waves of 'youth' rebellion. Most people who live through one have put themselves beyond the reach of the next by the time it comes along. But his experience, and the way that he reflects on it, gives some concrete examples of how flecks of memory, behaviour and cultural product can re-emerge in different contexts, sometimes having been carried there by individuals who've survived from one time to another.

The important role of mischief, humour and prank in counter-cultural rebellion was one of the key understandings Rimbaud carried over from the time of the Wallies to the provocations of punk. Accounts of the hoaxes which Crass perpetrated convey the power of Rimbaud's anarchist politics far better than the 'straight' political passages in this book. You don't have to appreciate the band's crude thrash rhythm, or the way their shouted lyrics often rely on sloganeering, blasphemy and the word fuck in order to cherish some of their finest achievements: their singles opposing the Malvinas/Falklands war, one of which was condemned in a House of Commons debate as 'the most vicious, scurrilous and obscene record that has ever been produced'; their release to the world press of a hoax taped private conversation between Reagan and Thatcher about the war, which was totally ignored until the USA Defence Department issued categorical denials that the tape was genuine, thereby alerting suspicion that perhaps there was 'something in it'; and the duping of *Total Loving* magazine to include a Crass rant against patriarchy and marriage on a compilation flexidisc of 'perfect songs to play on your wedding day'.

Throughout the book, there are references to the way Crass 'birthed a huge underground network of do-it-yourself activism, fanzines, record labels, activist action groups … ' Rimbaud and his publishers may be overstating the influence of Crass itself - they weren't the driving force in punk, but were part of a scene, which also included less attractive currents than those Crass came from. That's why they were sometimes fazed by sections of the audience they attracted, such as the skinheads who thought Crass's black clothes and logo suggested fascist allegiances. Nevertheless, the band's genuine commitment to counter-cultural values and stances did inspire and resource many who were to carry some of the values and outlooks of '67 and '77 through into the 1990s …

*AK Press are also publishing Rimbaud's novel* The Diamond Signature, *and* Crass Art, *a collection of collage and images by Gee Vaucher, the graphic designer who worked with the band on record sleeves, publications, posters and spray-paint graffiti stencils.*

# Public and private in sickness and in health

## Jude Rosen

John Diamond, C *because cowards get cancer too*, Vermilion, £6.99
*Out of It*, Simon Hattenstone, Sceptre £12.99
John Bayley, *Iris. A Memoir of Iris Murdoch*, Duckworth, £16.95
Hilary and Piers Du Pré, *A Genius in the Family. An Intimate Memoir of Jacqueline du Pré*, Vintage, £7,99
Linda Grant, *Remind Me Who I Am, Again*, Granta, £7.99

### The boundary between public and private

It all seemed so clear: 'the personal is political' was the stall feminism had set out in the 1970s. But the 'Diana phenomenon', and the Clinton/Lewinsky scandal have brought to a head great rifts in what feminists mean by the concept.

Is everything personal inherently political? Should everything private be exposed to public scrutiny? Should the public become the arbiter of personal behaviour?

Alongside these debates about the cultural shift in public revelation of private affairs, a new mode of self-expression has emerged - so-called 'confessional writing' - and here the waters are no less muddy. What are the politics of exposé and self-revelation? Or is it a question of taste? And are there political and ethical issues not only about the conduct of the media, but also of biographers and autobiographers?

One branch of the genre which highlights both strengths and pitfalls of the revelatory mode is the burgeoning literature on the experience of chronic or terminal illness, by the sufferers themselves or by their carers and loved ones. At last the unspoken voice of sufferers can talk back to the medical profession, to carers, to the indifferent and embarrassed, can tell what it feels like, can show the arbitrariness of the line between the healthy 'us' and the sick, or dying 'them'. It also offers a new voice to carers to explain the commitment and pain of caring.

The literature reviewed here is both poignant and problematic. It deals with a common currency of all humanity - mortality, impending or threatened - and at the same time how living with life-threatening disease challenges what it means to live. It is striking how many of these reflections are written by Jewish people and imbued with Jewish culture and humour. While these accounts leave largely untouched the dimension of class which so sharply correlates in our society with morbidity and mortality rates, they do raise questions of the power of the medical profession and the press, public ignorance and prejudice, private caring and emotional conflict, and the ethics of the representation of personal suffering.

Although the boundaries may be down, the ongoing distinction between public and private remains evident in these voices: it is the relationship between the two spheres that has to be resolved with due regard for both legitimate public interest and the dignity of the subject.

## The ethics of self-revelation: what is in the public interest?

At first sight, autobiography is not prone to the pitfalls of biography in violating privacy: the author, after all, *is* the subject. However, autobiography cannot be left off the hook when it comes to aesthetic choice - selecting only what is relevant and interesting, avoiding banality in recording insignificant details of lives. The ethical choice, which biographies and autobiographies have to confront, concerns the public interest. What is it in the public interest to reveal - and what should rightly remain private? The autobiographer of illness enters into a bargain with the reader - this is my story, this is how I felt it and this is how I see it. He or she owes it to the reader to be factually accurate journalistically and scientifically, to expose abuses of power and injustices, to attempt emotional honesty, to confront the conflicts and difficulties.

The two autobiographies, John Diamond's C *because cowards get cancer too* and the lesser known *Out of It* by Simon Hattenstone, both in their own way achieve a remarkable symbiosis - revealing inner anguish while pointing their fingers at public sores.

John Diamond, the former BBC producer and presenter, has followed the progress of his cancer, from neck cyst to tongue cancer to throat and neck cancer in his *Times* column, in a BBC documentary, and in this autobiography. It is in the Jewish tradition of 'kvetching' (as Matt Seaton so aptly observed of his late wife Ruth Picardie) - a kind of moaning-cum-messianic lament. Not that Diamond indulges in asking 'why me?' On the contrary, one of the most important public services he performs is in deriding views of cancer as punishment or redemptive experience. It is the cruel arbitrariness of the disease which his humour targets. In part, he writes as a therapeutic strategy to survive, but it becomes more than that. He acknowledges phases in his writing when he adopted a 'public denial therapy', feigning indifference or bravura, 'putting a jaunty spin on something depressing'. But the book rides above false rhetorical poses and acquires a different tone as he struggles to transform pain and potential death into ' best journalistic practice' - at its best, fine aesthetic form.

The unbearably poignant moment when he opened the letters and home-made cards of countless unknown readers who also are cancer sufferers, relatives or carers, and broke down, is testament to a new kind of private-public relationship. Diamond's lament began a dialogue between strangers, about the most terrible endurances of their lives. This constitutes journalism as public expression of private griefs, in a way which connects people suffering in isolation, and so comforts, informs about therapies and myths - thus clarifying choices, however hard - and allows rage and thus grieving. It is two-way - their acts of solidarity allow Diamond to express his pent-up emotion, just as his column had touched all these unknown fellow sufferers.

He demystifies the cancer both in explicit descriptions of symptoms and therapies - even showing the excised tongue tissue on TV - ridiculing the wild, unsustained claims of alternative therapies (perhaps with too much zeal - lumping together the charlatan and the serious, and confusing false claims of cures with real, if more limited relief). The list of contents of his medicine cupboard, which reads comically like an endless overstatement, becomes an inventory of his life as it is being lived now, a *reductio ad absurdum* of pills and pads and painkillers and the pity of it, because we know from the voice there is so much more to him than this.

The pitfall of self-pity is largely avoided through self-deprecating humour. All the way through, the obsessions of Jewish hypochondria, of schlemiel neuroses, of time wasting on endless introspection are sent up. They seem comical, contrasted with the harsh reality of the Diamond cancer.

## Tabloid representations of illness

The book also questions the tabloid press's representation of terminal illness in terms of bravery. He pinpoints one aspect of the press's voyeuristic portrayal of suffering as the triumph of innocence over evil, of the individual imbued with special qualities of courage against the odds. Thus it sentimentalises suffering, prettifying it as a moral tale which censors out the 'dirty realism' of dangerous, degrading disease. Diamond counters this, through genuinely modest but honest evaluation of his reactions to his illness, denying his special qualities or resources of character - indeed revelling in the opposite - not least in the self-deprecating title.

In the after-afterword to the paperback, 'The Last Word' - which announces the terminal spread of his cancer - Diamond insists that his is not confessional writing but reportage. He is not confessing, because cancer is not a sin to be ashamed of. Diamond shows that the subjectivity of the sick person, their inner world, can be as much a part of the investigation of illness, of reporting how it is, as the mechanics of disease. The effect of tabloid journalism, of perpetuating a sense of powerlessness to act against overwhelming forces, is countered by his sane, rational voice, his focus on what therapies do and how they have improved. Even where the choices are all nasty - between radiotherapy, chemotherapy, radical surgery or certain death - they are not meaningless. He shows a man using his intelligence and moral resources to ask questions, to come to terms with his emotions and make allowances when he fails, to gain some control over his fate.

## The child's voice

Simon Hattenstone's autobiographical account of his childhood encephalitis - inflammation - adopts a very different voice, largely that of a nine-year old boy, a bright, well-adjusted happy child in a Manchester Jewish family, who woke up one day with a terrible headache. This style of autobiographical reconstruction is novelistic in recreating a consistent reality in character and period with dialogues in register, excavating his inner mind as a child in a heightened state of being. In vivid, rumbustious scenes, he traces the phases of the illness and diagnosis over three years, through medical denial, abrupt termination of psychiatric treatment on discovery of a virulent streptococcal infection, to the encephalography which showed 'the tadpoles on his brain' - the antibody-telltales of the fight going on inside his head against the encephalitis - to his slow return to normality and the 'outside world'. Even though he had little energy to fight the disease, the narrative is full of energy, vividly portraying the passions, pain and psychological trauma of the boy, coming to terms with physical devastation and medical denial of his condition.

His language changes abruptly with the onset of the illness, and this is reflected in the blunt, frontal dialogue, designed to shock, and the garish prose, like an adolescent's bedroom. Hattenstone's pain combines the fluorescence of strobe lights with thumping bass: in his head, 'a wall of steel ... dropped between my ears and eyes'; the drilling and lightning white flashes turned his head into 'a building site'; his throat is 'mosquito bite itchy', 'callused', 'a sore gorge'; he shrank to 'xylophone ribs'; constipation left 'boulders in the belly'.

The memoir imaginatively recreates the reactions of a nine year old boy, then ten, then eleven, in his obsessive behaviour and routines: wild attachment to the glam rock bands of the era, over-identification with the lead figures - Marc Bolan and then Roy Wood, which gives the writing its period feel; making lists in his head of likes and dislikes - a calculus of whether it was worth living or not; making blasphemous contracts with God ... 'But if you do exist, please, please let me live, don't kill me, God because I want to live and be happy and be better, you vicious twat. Amen'.

It is ruthless in the portrayal through a child's eyes of the physical peculiarities and indignities of disease, his own and those of the other children in hospital. The cruelties are counterbalanced by the tenderness towards the other sick children in hospital and the alliances they form against the medics and the outside world, in defence of one another. The cruelty, combined with a surprising capacity for emotional connection comes out again in his brutal initiation into special school - 'for Mongs', where the boys who beat him up and douse him in shit are the same who later offer him a paper hanky - well, clean bog paper at least - to wipe his eyes on when he finally announces he has made it back to mainstream school.

*Out of it* gives voice to the child's experience of incomprehension at the hands of the GP, hospital doctors and psychiatrists who 'treated' him, and is a searing indictment of the medical profession's power: its failure to acknowledge fallibility, to listen to the child's inner desperation and explicit suffering, to apologise when it got it wrong. These attitudes not only left Simon Hattenstone undiagnosed and untreated for over a year, but infected the perceptions of people around him. The GP who called him 'a bleddy malingerer' was his father's best friend. The relatives who rallied round when he contracted pneumonia on top - because by then his immune system was so weak - knew how to react because they recognised the name of the illness, and its danger. Even Simon was cock-a-hoop at the diagnosis because at last he had a medical label and thus legitimacy for his condition. His book is a terrible testimony to the power of the medical profession to confer or withhold this legitimacy and thus also to provide or withhold appropriate treatment. It is also an indictment of moral judgement of the sick, and refusal to believe a child despite overwhelming physical evidence.

On the other hand, it is a paean of praise to the unlikeliest of friendships, mainly with older women, friends of his mother - a secretary who patiently typed up his book of song lyric-poems, a woman whose dog befriended the Hattenstones' dog in the park and so became a family friend. Marjorie Hattenstone adds an adult voice in the epilogue - which acts as a counterpoint to the narrative of the suffering child - thanking those who helped her son to recover: 'Ordinary people who recognised suffering whether it had a name or not.' The book draws the reader into the world of strange children - with drilling in their head, or outsize organs, or anorexic bodies, and lets you share what they feel.

These autobiographies show how self-revelatory writing about serious illness which operates with a sense of public concern can inform the public, enlarge its experience of suffering from different viewpoints, and act as a check on professional practice and power; thus it can have educative, sensitising and political effects. Such writing, at its best, can contribute to emotional literacy.

## The ethics of representation of others

While biography shares some of the same aesthetic problems as autobiography, it faces a special ethical problem in representing the illness of its subject, as s/he is not the author but another person - a close relative or loved one. There are numerous dangers of violating the dignity of the individual sufferer: by revealing too much, especially about the physical or mental degradation which the disease has wrought, or intimate details of their sex life before the illness struck; by being overwhelmed by the suffering inflicted on themselves in their caring role so that it eclipses the suffering of the sick person; by projecting the anger of unresolved family conflicts onto the subject, disfiguring the overall portrait. The most palpable danger in biography in this field, especially where the subject has impaired mental faculties or has died, is to deny the sufferer their voice and feelings.

It requires moral intelligence and a fine sense of judgement to avoid compounding the pain of a devastating illness with that of invasion of intimacy. Even where the person is not aware or is dead, the violation of memory causes pain to those who were close to the private person. Therefore, the biographer of the sick person has to tread very carefully. All the biographies reviewed here are problematic in this regard.

## The biography of the intimate other: Iris

John Bayley's biography of his wife, the novelist and philosopher Iris Murdoch, written while she was in an advanced state of Alzheimer's disease, but before she died, won general critical acclaim for its moving account of her condition, and his care for her. However, it is a slow, limp and unenlightening biography of her, lacking vitality and insight into her inner world, the sources of her creative thought and even their marriage. It positively revels in its psychological blindness, indeed elevates it to a virtue: 'What was she thinking? I had no idea … Such ignorance, such solitude - they suddenly seemed the best part of love and marriage. We were together because we were comforted and reassured by the solitariness each saw and was aware of in the other.'

Their early courtship is recounted with moments of cool eroticism as they slip into the river naked after their cycle rides round Oxford, but Bayley's account of his own emotions of anxiety and jealousy are nondescript. His memory lacks focus and so he goes into laborious details or irrelevant speculations. Not only does he convey his gaucheness in the courtship, but in his writing too. Iris is presented either in a childlike way - like a 'Watteau china doll' - or idealised as cerebral, untouched by the world, pure - 'this extraordinary creature', her many relationships 'innocent as in the garden of Eden'; when they finally get together, 'she babbled like a child and so did I ... With arms around each other, kissing and rubbing noses ... we rambled on seeming to invent on the spot ... a whole infantile language of our own.' He presents her as someone for whom sex was unimportant - and yet with many 'admirers' as he quaintly calls them, before their marriage. There is a tacky reminiscence about a dissatisfied admirer, indicating 'her shortcomings in bed'. The portrayal of their sex life retains the coyness and other-worldliness to show that Iris was contented with their quietistic marriage. He gives details of mentors with whom she allegedly just held hands, or whom she allowed to stroke her arms innocently while they had intense intellectual intercourse about poetry or the ancient world.

The same psychological naivety, idealisation and infantilisation shape the representation of Iris as an Alzheimer patient. What appears as physical awkwardness and naivety in confronting sexual feelings, jealousies and betrayals, becomes positively offensive in dealing with her suffering. His struggles to wash or dress her are supposed to be comic but the manner of their recounting is an unnecessary invasion of her body and person.

Only in the endlessly repeated refrain of 'When are we going? ' that weaves in and out of the text does he touch Iris's distress, and give a real measure of the disease's effect on her. The final part of the book, 'Now', is the only time the text really takes off and achieves authenticity of feeling. Its rather clipped diary form gives highlights and thus glimpses into his inner world, the tensions of covering up: 'the horrid wish to show others how bad things are'; the losses of temper and urgency of his own unmet needs: 'Wild wish to shout in her ear: "It's worse for me. It's much worse."' Yet these confessions have little intimation of understanding. The most vivid moment, when he flies into a rage with Iris, he describes in the third person, so out-of-touch is he with his own emotional turmoil - 'Astonishing how rage produces another person, who repels one, from whom one turns away in incredulous disgust, at the very moment one has become him and is speaking in his voice.' ... 'I find myself looking in a mirror at the man who has been speaking. A horrid face, plum colour.'

Thus at the end, the biography attains an emotional truth, not about Iris, but about John and the toll of the illness on him. But this was not the subject of the biography.

## Projection of unresolved emotional conflicts onto the other

The same problem recurs in A Genius in the Family. An Intimate Memoir of Jacqueline du Pré, by Hilary and Piers Du. The book is surprisingly well written, with a lively and informative portrait of their childhood and some of the sources of Jacqueline's - and indeed Hilary's - musical creativity, in particular their mother's use of Dalcroze eurhythmics to get them to form shapes and act out the colours of the music. But the biography is as blinkered as Bayley's in dealing with emotional conflicts - in this case the suppressed jealousies of sibling rivalry. It suffers from the most extraordinary psychological blindness, which colours its portrait of Jacqueline, indeed poisons it in some places.

Piers Du Pré reveals his sexual embarrassment at Jackie's revelations to him (somewhat bizarre in the circumstances) about using the (contraceptive) cap and later being invited to go swimming after one of her concerts in Berlin and finding they were skinny-dipping. The significance of his account of these events is that they are offered as proof of some moral relapse - from the innocence of their country home to the wanton ways of the world. His tone is judgmental as though something disgusting had happened. There is no psychological distance with which to analyse his earlier reactions as those of a sheltered adolescent. There is no adult voice or perspective on the past.

The note to the reader at the start sets out on a false premise - 'These are our memories. This book is not a biography, nor an account of Jackie's career. It is simply what happened.' The text includes excerpts of letters and dialogue between all the family members as adults, in which baby talk, childish nicknames, naive revelations, peevish hurts persist. Hilary Du Pré, who was progressing brilliantly in her own musical career as a flautist, until a poor relationship with a teacher at the Royal Academy precipitated a crisis of confidence about performing in public, blames Jacqueline for this change in her fortunes. In a number of the childhood scenes, she acknowledges the rivalry but declares she has overcome it. Yet the portrait of Jacqueline all the way through suffers from an ambivalence in the constant comparison between the two sisters. On the one hand Hilary envies Jacqueline - her own life would never be as exciting or glamorous as Jackie's, she had not gained equal public recognition, deep down she knew she was not as talented; on the other there is the one-up-man-ship - she had personal happiness and security, a husband, children, a beautiful country life and Jackie did not.

Such emotional ambivalence and suppressed resentment make it difficult to represent the ravages of Jacqueline's multiple sclerosis with any kind of equanimity. Hilary tries. She reaches back into the past to seek to identify the first signs of the disease, which Jacqueline kept from her family. She tries to make links between the deterioration in her behaviour, particularly the breakdown which led to the affair with Hilary's husband, and the early onset of symptoms. But this is retrospective, at the end of the book. Both she and her brother tend to highlight unresolved hurts in order to blame, and thus exculpate themselves. The need to do so is not so much real (who are we to judge?) as psychological, set up by the suppression of negative feelings, which are then overcompensated for by loud proclamations of love and claims to privileged knowledge of the 'real' Jacqueline. In the process, the inner suffering of the real Jacqueline escapes from view. Again, the biography succeeds in illuminating unwittingly the inner world and interactions of the biographers, but far less so that of its main subject.

## Memory and self

Linda Grant's fine memoir of her Liverpool Jewish background and her mother's descent into dementia illustrates the ethical dilemma of representing the subject who has no right of reply. Although the author explicitly agonises over the ethics of biographical representation, she does not seem aware of the key problem - the projection of her own childhood anger and dislike of her mother on to the portrait of her mental deterioration which is disturbing and demeaning. Her mother is unable to counteract it or give her side of the story. At the same time, Grant depicts how impossible her mother was and is, so as to justify and explain why she cannot live with her and care for her full-time. Guilt and self-justification almost become the driving force of the narrative with the tendency to objectify her mother, failing to get inside her contradictory motivations, actions and feelings.

The difficulties of these biographies illustrates the value of fiction in portrayal of illness. The virtue of fictionalisation lies in forcing the writer to give voice to the other, without which the character cannot live. Where the biographical subject in real life may have lost full mental awareness or be dead, in the novel they can be brought back to conscious life. Fiction universalises, enabling us to see and hear other voices from the inside as well as the outside. It also builds up multifold characterisation by showing a character in many interactions with others. This can therefore give a full characterisation to a sick person, as well as their carers and loved ones and build a more complex truth than that of a single perspective

However, Linda Grant's memoir also seeks to link personal to collective memory, in a sophisticated way. She is far too good a writer not to try to locate the individual tragedy in family and group history, to partake of that two-way traffic which feminism sought to establish between subjectivity and social situation. Yet, in the desire to move away from a naive picture of her own truth-telling, she has adopted an overly post-modern conception of memory which blurs its relationship to history and the line between reinvention of self and conscious lying about past. The problematic aspects of her mother - the cover-up of origins, trying to forget, rose-tinting her memories, were not features of all immigrants remaking their lives. It is important to separate historical reconstruction from personal memory - for while personal memories are an important source for historians, they are only raw material which has to be sifted and analysed for its partiality, ellipses, repressions, silences, which are themselves instructive about the political and cultural climate and what Raymond Williams called 'the structure of feeling'. They may tell us what was permissible and impermissible for an aspiring young woman in the upwardly mobile Jewish lower middle class of Liverpool; they may give insight into the snobbery and showiness which were the bounds of aspiration for such a woman in the absence of the realisation of Jewish immigrants' social dreams. But her reconstruction of self does not exhaust the real field of possibilities which were available to Jewish women of that generation and class.

This conflation of memory and history is linked to a second problem. Grant reinforces the concept of permanent revolution of the self with a bio-chemical portrait of memory as firing neurones and synaptic lapses. But this concept of a constant reconstruction of self gives too much weight to the idea of self as purely project, rather than as a process where a degree of consciousness always meets the barriers of the fossilised, internalised past and the material limits of the present. We may choose to remake ourselves, but it is always with historically inherited and contextually restricted material. We don't start with a clean slate.

There are, clearly, some problems with this book. Nevertheless Grant paints a powerful portrait of life strains and contradictions, and offers important insights into some of the sources of Jewish eccentricity, and the psychological distress that can lead to or accompany madness.

## Storming the Millennium
## The New Politics of Change
*Edited by Tim Jordan and Adam Lent*

**Recommended retail price £12.99.
Available to *Soundings* readers for
£10.99 post free.**

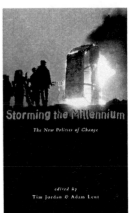

As the new millennium begins, activists are
reflecting on their struggles, and journalists and
intellectuals are recognising the importance of the new politics of change.
*Storming the Millennium* is the first book to bring a range of activists and
intellectuals together and it provides some of the first histories of
movements at the core of new politics, grappling with the important
political and theoretical issues they raise.

Bringing together new and established writers, *Storming the Millennium*
includes discussions of crime and justice, disabilities, bisexual, gay,
lesbian and transgender politics, race issues in 1990s Britain and
activism on the Internet. It also addresses the relationship between new
politics, the new left and socialism.

**Contributors:** Peter Beresford, Tessa Bird, Patrick Field, Tony Fitzpatrick,
Nancy Fraser, Stuart Hall, Shirin Housee, Rupa Huq, Tim Jordan, Adam
Lent, Doreen Massey, Michael Rustin, Sanjay Sharma, Merl Storr.

# Transversal Politics

# Transversal politics and translating practices

## Cynthia Cockburn and Lynette Hunter

'Transversal politics' is a term that does not have wide currency in English. It has reached us from Italian women peace activists, networking with women in other countries, who talk about their practice of *politica trasversale*. But, among the projects described in this thematic section of *Soundings*, its use has been

growing. It seems as if it has fallen, clunk, upon a meaning that has been waiting for a signifier. It answers to a need to conceptualise a democratic practice of a particular kind, a process can on the one hand look for commonalities without being arrogantly universalist, and on the other affirm difference without being transfixed by it. Transversal politics is the practice of creatively crossing (and re-drawing) the borders that mark significant politicised differences. It means empathy without sameness, shifting without tearing up your roots. Nira Yuval-Davis has more to say about this in 'What is "transversal politics"?' (p94).

These pages bring together writings invoked by two consecutive conferences held at Gresham College, London, on 29-30 January 1999. The first day was called 'Doing Transversal Politics' and the second 'Translating Words', 'Translating Practices'. The link between the two days was of itself something of a conceptual boundary crossing, a sideways leap in the dark.

T he 'Doing Transversal Politics' conference marked the conclusion of research by Cynthia Cockburn, begun in 1995. The title of the research was Women Building Bridges, and it involved studying how certain women's projects, in countries where there was war, created and sustained their alliances across difficult ethno-national differences.[1]

The three projects sent representatives to the Gresham conferences. The first, Medica Women's Association in Bosnia-Hercegovina, is a therapy centre that responds with medical and psycho-social care to women and children traumatised by war and post-war violence. In Medica the Bosnian Muslim majority have worked throughout the war and the ensuing uneasy peace alongside a remaining minority of women who are of Bosnian Serb, Bosnian Croat and mixed backgrounds. From Medica, Ajli Bajramovic and Rada Stakic-Domuz attended the seminars.

The second project is Bat Shalom, a group of Israeli Jewish and Israeli Palestinian Arab women living in northern Israel, who campaign together for

---

1. The Women Building Bridges research project was funded by City University, the E. and H.N. Boyd and J.E. Morland Charitable Trust, the William A. Cadbury Charitable Trust, the Community Relations Commission of Northern Ireland, the Global Fund for Women, the Lipman-Miliband Trust, the Network for Social Change, the Niwano Peace Foundation, the Scurrah Wainwright Charity and Womankind Worldwide.

justice and peace in the region. Bat Shalom was represented by Samira Khouri and Sonia Zarchi, accompanied by Vera Jordan.

The third project of Women Building Bridges is the Women's Support  Network, Belfast, represented by May McCann and Maura McCrory, accompanied by Marie Mulholland, the former coordinator. The Network is a cross-community alliance of women's centres and other women's organisations that have come together to get working-class women's needs voiced in the political system and the peace process of Northern Ireland.[2]

During 1998 the three projects made a further transversal move, exchanging visits across state boundaries to see what could be learned from each other's experience.[3] It was the findings of this series of transnational visits (we called this continuation of the project Bridge Between Bridges) that were presented at the 'Doing Transversal Politics' conference. Representing the workings of an ethnically mixed project is difficult. But representing a prolonged interaction between such complex unities is more challenging yet. So we tried to do this at the conference by showing analytical videos of the exchange visits, each one framed by a panel discussion with some of the women involved (see 'Crossing Borders' (p99)).

This however does not exhaust the transversal steps we were into here. The first day was in fact a partnership between Women Building Bridges and Southall Black Sisters. SBS was founded twenty years ago by Asian and African-Caribbean women and has become well-known for practical and campaigning work on issues of domestic violence and racism. They are today effectively an

---

2. Photo-narratives about these three projects were published in *Soundings* as 'Different Together', Issue 2, Spring 1996; 'Refusing Ethnic Closure', Issue 3, Summer 1996; and 'Wrong and wrong again', Issue 5, Spring 1997. The research is reported in full in Cynthia Cockburn, *The Space Between Us: Negotiating Gender and National Identities in Conflict*, Zed Books, London 1998.
3. For the funding of this second phase of the research we are indebted to Gresham College, the Global Fund for Women, the Network for Social Change and the Scurrah Wainwright Charity.

alliance of women of Hindu, Moslem, Sikh and other cultural backgrounds. Their transversal moves, explored by Pragna Patel in her article 'Difficult Alliances' (p115), involve handling conflictual ethnic differences constituted in the Indian sub-continent and reformulated in Britain. They describe the tactical alliances they have to make with, among others, conservative community leaders and an often misogynist anti-racist movement.

In stepping into partnership for a day, Southall Black Sisters and Women Building Bridges were attempting to share experiences of holding together alliances in different violent contexts. For Medica, Bat Shalom and the Women's Support Network the situation is one of war or its aftermath. Southall Black Sisters are surviving situations in Britain of diasporic tension and urban racism that sometimes seem like war. Both fields of violence are of course gendered.

The art of transversal politics is a perennial scepticism about 'community'. It means knowing that when community is invoked it is often to plaster over cracks and deny differences within. At the same time it also means refusing to let go of the idea that constructive dialogue and shared actions are possible. It is a tolerance of distinctiveness which is at the same time an intolerance of non-communication. Metaphorically and actually this means multi-lingualism. It is about foregoing the dream of finding a common tongue (because, given power relations, that is bound to be an imperialism)  and instead taking up the challenge of learning each other's languages.

So it makes sense that the conference that was twinned with 'Doing Transversal Politics' was about 'Translating Words' 'Translating Practices'. And our participants, a healthy mix of activists and academics, seemed to have confidence in a meaningful connection between the two days, for more than half of those who came to the first day were also present at the second.[4]

---

4. Gresham College was both the sponsor and the host of the two conferences described here. (Lynette Hunter is current holder of the Gresham College Chair of Rhetoric). They also funded a partnership between Lynette and Cynthia Cockburn in the context of which the latter carried through the Bridge Between Bridges exchanges.

The 'Translating' conference resulted from a collaboration between Lynette Hunter and Rebecca O'Rourke. Lynette's focus is new writings in English, and as a teacher she is concerned with democratic access to communication. Likewise Rebecca's experience is in community writing and publishing and in adult education. They share a belief that good communicating is a strong mode for political agency. Whether in writing or speaking, we use words to write or speak ourselves into existence. They would ask: what encourages and enables communication across difficult differences of location, culture and political belief? How can we communicate to someone differently situated what it is like to experience war, survive uprooting or torture, or live in a society of ingrained violence and brutality? Can we translate into another language or culture, or from the spoken to the written word, without differences of power between us distorting what we say? They talk about their work in 'The Values of Community Writing' (p144).

The 'Translating' conference included speakers with experience in devising verbal strategies for dealing with ethnic, religious, cultural or political differentiation, division and oppression. There was Theatre and Reconciliation, an innovatory community theatre project developed in Northern Ireland, Eritrea and other African countries. Rather than making a speech, Gerri Moriarty and Jane Plastow involved the participants in a demonstration of how theatre can be used for empowerment, for gaining a voice. (See 'Theatre and Reconciliation' (p153).

There was MAMA, represented by Amina Souleiman and Saynab Osman. This is a story telling and writing project from which several books have issued, involving women who are refugees from Somalia and other East African countries now living in Sheffield. (See *Sharing Stories* (p163). Sonia Linden, writer in residence at the Medical Foundation for the Care of Victims of Torture, read an account by Nasrin Parveez, who was sitting beside her, of the brutality inflicted on her during imprisonment in Iran. It seemed that no-one in the room was able draw a breath as they took in this narrative. But having found words to tell about the torture, it no longer, Nasrin said, invades her sleep as nightmare.

Other presentations at the 'Translating' conference included Celia Hunt and Urmila Sinha, both developing and teaching the therapeutic use of creative writing, and East Side Arts, a bookshop-based community arts and people's history project based in Whitechapel, in East London. They told how they have found working with words can help individuals, small groups and migrant communities deal with urban racism and domestic violence. Emily Clark and Fran Duncan came from a Gypsy and Traveller project in Cleveland and spoke at the conference about how storytelling is used by women to deal with the discrimination and violence inflicted on the community by the wider society. They talked about links they have forged between non-settled peoples in the UK, France, Sweden and Denmark.

The women who came to the 'Translating' conference share a belief that skills of reading, writing and speaking, which are also part of daily life, are an important strategy for agency for those who are persistently muffled and marginalised. The same skills are needed for handling difference. In the 'Transversal Politics' event the day before, Pragna Patel had told the story of the moment when inter-communal violence in the Indian subcontinent had increased tensions between Muslim and Hindu women in Southall Black Sisters to the point of rupture. The words she found to describe that crisis were, precisely: 'We were lost for words'.

---

## Urgent Appeal
# MEDICA KOSOVA

Medical and psycho-social care for women traumatized by rape and other forms of terror in the expulsions from Kosova. Drawing on our experience in Bosnia, we are women training women in appropriate responses to sexual violence. We are setting up tent clinics and a mobile unit. And beginning documentation of violations of women's human rights. Your help will reach us without delay. Cheques, please, to:

### 'Medica', PO Box 9560, London NW5 2WF.

---

# What is 'transversal politics'?

## Nira Yuval-Davis

Nira Yuval-Davis *provides a brief introduction to the concept of transversal politics.*

Like many other feminist activists, I have been in search of a name for what so many of us are doing.[1] I found it when I was invited by Italian feminists from Bologna to a meeting they organised between Palestinian and Israeli (both Jewish and Palestinian) women which took place in 1993. I later learned that there has been a whole tradition of autonomous left politics in Bologna under the name of transversal politics.

Before describing what transversal politics is, it is important to state what it is not. Transversal politics has been developed as an alternative to the assimilationist 'universalistic' politics of the Left on the one hand, and to identity politics on the other hand. While the first has proved to be ethnocentric and exclusionary, the second has proved to be essentialist, reifying boundaries between groups and, by homogenising and collapsing individual into collective identities, undemocratic within groups.

Transversal politics is based on the following. First, standpoint epistemology, which recognises that from each positioning the world is seen differently, and

---

1. E.g. 'unity in diversity' - see Nira Yuval-Davis, 'Identity politics and women's ethnicity' in V.M. Moghadam (ed), *Identity Politics and Women*, Westview Press, Bolder, Co 1994; and Kumari Jawayardena, *The White Woman Other Burden: Western Women and South Asia during British Rule*, Routledge, London 1995, p10.

thus that any knowledge based on just one positioning is 'unfinished' - which is not the same thing as saying it is 'invalid'.[2] In this epistemology, the only way to approach 'the truth' is by a dialogue between people of differential positionings.

Secondly, an important concept in relation to transversal politics is the encompassment of difference by equality.[3] This means the recognition, on the one hand, that differences are important (as stated in the foregoing paragraph), but on the other hand, that notions of difference should encompass, rather than replace, notions of equality. Such notions of difference are not hierarchical. They assume *a priori* respect for others' positionings - which includes acknowledgement of their differential social, economic and political power.

Thirdly, transversal politics is based on a conceptual - and political - differentiation between positioning, identity and values. People who identify themselves as belonging to the same collectivity or category can be positioned very differently in relation to a whole range of social divisions (e.g. class, gender, ability, sexuality, stage in the life cycle etc). At the same time, people with similar positioning and/or identity, can have very different social and political values.

Several implications can be drawn from the above. One is that feminist and other community activists should not see themselves as representatives of their constituencies (unless they were democratically elected and are accountable for their actions). Rather, they should see themselves as their advocates, working to promote their cause. However, even as advocates, it is important that the activists should be conscious of the multiplexity of their specific positionings, both in relation to other members in their constituencies, as well as in relation to the other participants in the specific encounter. One of the problems with both identity politics and - probably even more importantly - with multiculturalist policies, is that such activists and 'community leaders' too often become the 'authentic voice' of their communities. This is often, as Pragna Patel points out in her article in this volume (see p115) harmful to women and other marginal elements within these communities.

---

2. Donna Haraway, 'Situated knowledge: The science question in feminism and the privilege of partial perspective', *Feminist Studies* 14(3), 1988.
3. See Louis Dumont, *Homo Hierarchicus*, Paladin, New York 1972; for Pnina Werbner and Nira Yuval-Davis, 'Women and the new discourse of citizenship', in N. Yuval-Davis and P. Werbner (eds), *Women, Citizenship and Difference*, Zed Books, London 1999.

A second implication is that such advocates do not necessarily or always have to be members of that constituency. It is the message, not the messenger that counts. This does not mean, of course, that it is immaterial who the 'messenger' is. The feminists in Bologna introduced the concepts of 'rooting' and 'shifting' to clarify how this could be done. The idea is that each such 'messenger', and each participant in a political dialogue, would bring with them the reflexive knowledge of their own positioning and identity. This is the 'rooting'. At the same time, they should also try to 'shift' - to put themselves in the situation of those with whom they are in dialogue and who are different.

Transversal politics, nevertheless, does not assume that the dialogue is without boundaries or that each conflict of interest is reconcilable - although, as Jindi Pettman points out 'there are almost always possibilities for congenial or at least tolerable personal, social and political engagements'.[4] Similar, compatible values can cut across differences in positionings and identity and assume what Alison Assiter calls 'epistemological communities'.[5] Such epistemological communities share common value systems, and can exist across difference. The struggle against oppression and discrimination might, and mostly does, have a specific categorical focus but is never confined just to that category.

What the boundaries of the feminist 'epistemological community' and coalition politics should be is a difficult question, not only because the specific historical conditions in which any specific feminist campaign might be carried out can vary so much, but also because there are so many strands among self-identified feminists, among whom there may be very serious divisions of opinions. Moreover, as Angela Davis herself has pointed out, if the struggle against her imprisonment in the 1970s had been limited only to those who shared her politics, the campaign would have never been successful. And this is true of many other campaigns. Also, not all political campaigns are the same. There are different levels of overlapping value systems and different levels of common political work, from a tight formal organisation to a loose informal network, from an ideological alliance to a single-issue-based coalition.

---

4. Jan Pettman, *Living in the margins, racism, sexism and feminism in Australia*, Allen & Unwin, Sydney 1992, p157.
5. Alison Assiter, *Enlightened Women: Modernist Feminism in a Postmodern Age*, Routledge, London 1996, chpt 5.

However, this multiplicity of forms and intensities of coalition politics should not make us all into post-modern 'free floating signifiers' for whom 'anything goes'. Transversal politics stop where the proposed aims of the struggle are aimed at conserving or promoting unequal relations of power, and where essentialised notions of identity and difference naturalise forms of social, political and economic exclusion. The processes of 'shifting' and 'rooting' can help to distinguish between differences that are of context and terminology

'too often "community leaders" become the "authentic voice" of their communities'

and differences that are of values and goals. This can have very little to do with labels and stereotypes of 'Otherness'.

During the last ten or fifteen years, there has been a lot of progress, locally and globally, in what Charles Taylor called 'the politics of recognition'.[6] One of the effects of this has been a growing decentering of the West and a much wider and equal dialogue between feminist and other activists on a global scale. The travel and communication revolutions, especially the growing use of the Internet, have played central roles in this development. The various UN NGO forums as they have developed in Rio, Vienna, Cairo, Copenhagen and Beijing have seen many examples of transversal dialogue and co-operation. The recent UNIFEM videoed conference on violence against women (which took place on International Women's Day, 8 March 1999) combined the technical, organisational and political advances of this movement. Probably even more impressive have been the dialogues and co-operation that have been taking place among women's and peace organisations from opposing sides of ethnic and national conflicts. On a more local level, organisations like Women Against Fundamentalisms, and Justice For Women, have been able to work in a way in which differences encompassed equality among their members without falling into the pitfall of identity politics (see reference to Women Against Fundamentalisms in Marie Mulholland and Pragna Patel's article in this journal, p134).

In many ways, the political dialogue in Northern Ireland and the proposed political settlement (whose fate, unfortunately, at the time of writing, seems

6. Taylor, Charles, 'Examining the Politics of Recognition', in Amy Gutmann (ed), *Multiculturalism*, Princeton University Press, Princeton 1994.

97

more and more in doubt) have reflected the beginning of a shift in 'establishment politics' too towards transversal politics. However, as important and positive as transversal politics is, there is a silence/absence at its heart which would need confronting and transcending before it could successfully move into the centre of the political stage.

Transversal politics recognises the differential power positions among participants in the dialogue, but it nevertheless encompasses these differences with equal respect and recognition of each participant. Moreover, transversal politics resists autocratic decision-making mechanisms in which certain individuals take upon themselves to 'represent' their communities. However, it does not offer any alternative mechanism or criterion for decision-making, especially in times and places where the old feminist ideal of consensus politics is unavailable or impractical. Moreover, because transversal politics does not privilege *a priori* any positioning or identity, the same value system might simultaneously prioritise different political projects from different standpoints. For example, where campaigns about women's control of their own bodies might prioritise struggles for the legalisation of abortion in one location, they might prioritise against forced sterilisation in another. This is not important if both struggles can take place at the same time with mutual support. However, if there are only limited human and financial resources available and there is a need to choose only one of these struggles at any one time, there is no built-in transversal way of deciding which one to choose. This was one of the main reasons that a transversal organisation like Women Against Fundamentalism could at a certain point become paralysed.

To sum up, then, transversal politics represents in many ways an important advance on the earlier *modus operandi* of the Left, which fell into traps of 'over' universalism or 'over' relativism. However, for transversal politics to become a major tool of 'real politics' as well as of 'alternative' social movements, requires from us more thinking and doing.

*This article derives from a ten minute introduction to 'transversal politics' given at the seminar 'Doing Transversal Politics' in January 1999. It is therefore very brief and schematic. I have elaborated more on the concept in my article 'Women, ethnicity and empowerment', in* Feminism and Psychology, *special issue, Shifting identities, shifting racisms, edited by K. Bhavnani and A Phoenix; and in my book* Gender and Nation, *Sage, London 1997, chs. 4 & 6).*

# Crossing borders

## Comparing ways of handling conflictual differences

## Cynthia Cockburn

Cynthia Cockburn *describes some of the collaborations of the Women Building Bridges Project.*

There are places and times when our differences are nothing but enrichment. And there are places and times when they bring us to the brink of mutual annihilation. In the three countries traversed by the Women Building Bridges project, described in the foregoing introduction, ethno-national identities are not things you can treat as options, flirt with, or use in dressing-up games. In Northern Ireland, Bosnia-Hercegovina and Israel/Palestine they have become things people are prepared to kill and die for.

The three projects, the Women's Support Network in Belfast, Medica in Bosnia and Bat Shalom in northern Israel, all embody versions of these dangerous differences within themselves and have each found their way towards defining them less threateningly and holding them together, for purposes of the work they have decided to do, in a shared project identity.

Having initially made each other's acquaintance in 1996, two years later the three projects embarked on an exchange of visits to share experience on how they do their work as (and for) women in violent situations, and in particular on how they handle conflictual differences within the projects. This article first briefly delineates the particular national conflicts within which the projects exist, and the constituent ethnic collectivities, and says something about

the nature of the three projects. It then goes on to recount some of the issues that came up between them when they travelled to each other's places. In this I draw on the script of videos we made during the visits, with the idea of carrying back home, to those who were not among the travellers, just what had been the substance of the interaction during the trips. The article concludes by drawing out some of the very real difficulties in practical solidarity work across barriers of language, culture, geography and political system - even when

*Video still from visit to Ireland. All subsequent stills are from exchange visits*

peace is the prize, and even when gender is removed as a variable.

There is little need, perhaps, to recall that there is a long history of conflict in Ireland, in which Britain has been implicated as a colonising power. It is also well known that partition of the island in 1921, eventually enabling the emergence of an independent Republic in the South, left the North as a Protestant-dominated province of the UK, with a dissatisfied Catholic minority.

The present war dates from the emergence of a civil rights movement in Northern Ireland in the late 1960s. The British government responded to the resulting violence by imposing direct rule. A three-way conflict has ensued between a heavy handed and partial British state, Republicans (mainly Catholic) some of whom are prepared to use force to unite the north with the Irish Republic, and Loyalists (mainly Protestant) some of whom are prepared to use force to resist this.

The 'troubles' as they are euphemistically called, have made of Belfast a violence-prone and impoverished city, a chequer-board of clearly demarcated neighbourhoods either predominantly nationalist/Catholic or unionist/

Protestant. The segregated communities, to a greater or lesser extent controlled by sectarian parties and paramilitary groups, have often been in fear of each other.

The Women's Support Network spans Belfast's two ethno-political communities. It is an umbrella organisation clustering seven territorially-based women's centres and a number of other women's groups. Their aim is to get a better deal, in terms of political recognition and funding, for working-class women who, they point out, are the most excluded group in a viciously divided society. They also campaign for principles of equality and inclusion in peace-making and policy-making in Northern Ireland. The Network aspires to achieve this focused alliance without its members having to drop or deny their very real differences in tradition and political belief. Its members call it 'a united feminist voice *affirming* difference'.

National identities in Bosnia, as in Ireland, are largely an artefact of politics. To distinguish somebody as Serb, Croat or Muslim is to ignore centuries of proximity, intermarriage and cultural flux. But when the federal Yugoslav state, due partly to external factors, became destabilised in the late 1980s, ethno-national identities were manipulated and mutually antagonised by leaders seeking material and political advantage. The result is well known: secession, ethnic aggression and warfare, then separatism.

In its day-to-day work, Medica Women's Association differs substantially from the Women's Support Network. It is a therapy centre that provides gynaecological and psycho-social care to women refugees and their children, and it began as a resource particularly for the many women who were raped in the war. Its 60-strong Bosnian staff include doctors, nurses and psychotherapists, cooks and carers, administrators, teachers and trainers.

The devastating forced movements of population of 1992-5 created of central Bosnia, where Medica is situated, a Muslim enclave. So in Medica the great majority of the women staff, like the refugees they care for, are Bosnian Muslims. There are however still 10 per cent or so of Bosnian Serb, Bosnian Croat, Slovenian or other background, and more who are of mixed parentage or in mixed marriages. All these women share the loss of a common Yugoslav identity, and they all chose to resist the wave of nationalist fear and hatred and remain loyal to the idea of a democratic and mixed society, Bosnia if not Yugoslavia. Unlike the Women's Support Network, then, where the alliance is a consciously constructed one, Medica's mixity is residual. And in terms of constitutional politics (though not in terms of embittering war-time experiences) its women have less to currently divide them than those of the Network.

In Israel/Palestine the principal issue of the war is the recognition as an autonomous Palestinian state of the territories occupied by Israel on the West Bank of the Jordan and the Gaza strip. As in N.Ireland and Bosnia, there is ostensibly a peace agreement providing for phased steps towards this constitutional outcome. But the war here continues regardless of the Oslo Accords and the unresolved injustices of the situation are painfully evident. Encroachment of Jewish settlers onto Palestinian land continues, with the Israeli authorities apparently complicit. Attacks on Israel by Palestinian refugee communities in southern Lebanon and elsewhere continue, met by large-scale actions of the Israeli Defence Forces.

When the Israeli state was established in 1948 it involved the exile of three-quarters of a million Palestinians. A minority however remained inside the borders of the new state as internal refugees. Today they and their offspring are

18 per cent of the Israeli population. Bat Shalom is a mixed group of peace activists from among these Israeli Palestinian Arabs and their Jewish neighbours, campaigning for justice and an end to the violence and militarisation of the two societies. The women involved in Women Building Bridges were members of a particular branch of Bat Shalom in the area around Megiddo, Nazareth and The Valleys on the southern edge of Galilee.

Unlike the Catholics and Protestants of N. Ireland and the various Bosnian ethnic groups, who are not noticeably different in dress or language, Jews and Arabs in Israel are of sharply differentiated cultures. The Jewish women are in the main members of rural kibbutzim. They tend to be secular, collective and anti-consumerist. The Palestinian Arab members of the project are of both Christian and Muslim background, and they and their families make their livelihood under very different conditions, in a competitive economy and a discriminatory labour market. All but the older generation of Arabs in Israel today speak Hebrew, but very few Jews have learned Arabic.

In organising the 1998 exchange visits, the Women's Support Network was the lynchpin. During June and July the Network received a group of Medica women, and sent a group of its own to Bosnia in return. And in the autumn months the Network exchanged visits with women from Bat Shalom. In each case there were four travellers - who at home also acted as the principal hosts. And in each case the journeys lasted two weeks.

The programmes were very full, physically and emotionally exhausting. They involved staying in each other's homes, getting to make friends; immersion in the life and work of the host project; visits to other sites in the geographical vicinity, and to other projects in the political vicinity. They also included intense workshops and seminars to deal with issues in greater depth and to compare and contrast their practices. And of course a lot of partying.

Maura McCrory, Gillian Gibson, Edel Quinn and Margaret Smith, who visited Medica's home town, Zenica, in central Bosnia, were deeply moved to be in the war zone that had filled their television screens not so long ago. Two years had done little to mend the destruction, for very many shelled and burned out villages and suburban areas are still abandoned and likely to remain so. And every place has its story of expulsion, murder and rape.

Edel said,

> The first thing that struck me was the devastation. Even the first night ... We arrived and it was pitch dark and we could see the silhouettes of buildings and we were getting a guide - like, 'this is where this was blown up, this is where these people were massacred'. And we couldn't see it. And in a way I was glad we couldn't see it. Because I was upset just at the sense of it.

Zenica was a government stronghold during the war, and the town itself was relatively unscathed. But it took in 70,000 refugees, so that its flats and houses are overcrowded and there are still many hope-abandoned camps in the area. The four visitors were also taken to visit Gornji Vakuf, a Muslim/Croat town that tore itself in two along the line of the high street. They saw Mostar, where a gesture of cosmetic reconstruction of the historic centre by foreign donors cannot hide the brutality of the Croat bombardment of the Muslim half of the town. And you do not easily forget the aching space over the river Neretva left by the mediaeval bridge, the Stari Most, now blasted to rubble in the gorge.

You somehow get hardened to your own local hostilities. The sight of somebody else's war disturbs the settled relationship you have to yours. Gillian said to the Bosnian women as she left, 'I think people in Bosnia really understand what I say. I don't know if it's the same for you ... sometimes in trying to make sense of your situation we're really making sense of our own'. They went back to Belfast feeling a little differently about home. They felt 'we could have been like Bosnia, this could still happen to us'.

The Belfast women had been particularly struck by the way the Medica psychotherapists talk about war 'trauma' in Bosnia. One of them said,

> I think we diminish our situation by not using it. We have never talked about suffering trauma, never. That's a word Bosnian people have the right to use, because they've lived through a war. But someone in Northern Ireland who had a relative shot or was the victim of a bomb explosion would be called 'victims'. So trauma's a word that I think we'll begin to use.

They were more clear now that what they have had in Northern Ireland has really been a war, not just the nasty little scrap so often diminished as 'the troubles'.

The four Network members to visit Israel/Palestine that autumn were May McCann, Julie Murray, Amanda Verlaque and Joanne Vance. They were deeply shaken by the experience. They had not expected the heavy security they would meet at the airport, the in-your-face militarisation of the country. They were not ready for the contrasts of wealth and poverty they were going to see, the luxury homes in Tel Aviv, dismal apartment blocks where newly arrived immigrants are lodged. But the most disturbing thing was the political turmoil, the fear, the open anger both among Palestinian Arabs and extreme elements of the Jewish community.

The Bat Shalom women took them across the Green Line to visit women in Jenin, in the Occupied Territories. They quickly realised that, yes, Israel and Northern Ireland are both settler societies, there are issues of land and language, borders and state-making in both regions. But that hardly means the road to peace here is the Belfast road. Or that peace is even in sight. In the British Isles the two governments now want a constitutional agreement. Israel is ruled by unremitting hawks.

But perhaps the hardest thing to take was the disadvantage of the Arabs within Israel. Here again there was a difference with Northern Ireland, where Catholic demands for civil rights have been listened to. Israel is defined as a state of the Jewish people, not a state of its citizens. So non-Jews are constitutionally unequal. Particularly painful is the land issue. Everywhere the women went in Galilee and the Triangle they saw what it meant: the Palestinians dispossessed of their properties in 1948, the establishment of Jewish kibbutzim and towns on the land they took over, and the law that has since prohibited Arabs from buying agricultural land and keeps them holed up in ever more crowded towns and villages.

They had read about all this in the newspapers back home, but tucked it away out of reach of feelings. Once in Israel, bitterness against the Zionist project boiled over. It is more comfortable to forget that there are different versions of Zionism, and to forget also the historic injustices Europe inflicted on the Jews of the diaspora, providing a rationale for a Jewish homeland.

I felt it in myself too, a deep desire for everyone to be of like mind on the 'simple' fact of Israeli oppression. But what we learned with Bat Shalom is that the virtue of an alliance lies precisely in holding together people who are of not-quite-like mind. It is relatively easy for an anti-Zionist Jew to work with Arabs. It is much harder, and very unusual, for a Zionist to look for what common purpose may exist with Palestinians, and once it is found, come out on the public highroad in defence of it.

Just before May went home, with a visit to the Holocaust memorial museum fresh in her mind, she said, 'In the historical context I completely understand the fear and the negative stereotyping. And the war, totally raw and open and near. And potentially going to happen again. They're nowhere near peace. And so I just think they're extremely brave women. I thought that at the beginning and nothing that I've learned, the complexities of what I've learned, has taken it away.'

V isiting Northern Ireland, if you are Bosnian or Israeli, is a strangely disquieting experience. It all seems so normal at first. In contrast to the millions uprooted and hundreds of thousands dead in the Yugoslav wars, in contrast to the massive mobilisation and high stakes in the Middle East conflict, the Northern Ireland war, a thing of side streets and country lanes, is almost invisible. This is especially so now that, for the moment, most of the British army saracens and foot patrols are back in barracks.

What struck the visitors most was the way a low intensity war can result in maximal mistrust and segregation among ordinary people. Ajli Bajramovic, Aida Arnaut, Amira Frljak and Selena Tufek from Medica visited the different women's centres in the Falls Road and the Shankill, in Poleglass and Windsor,

 saw the way every kerbstone and lamp-post carries its sectarian colour-markings, the way the Republican, and even more the Loyalist, murals and graffiti on street walls and gable ends insist on the thinkability of killing.

And as they went back to Bosnia, Aida said, 'This way of living, separate schools, separate groups - it's a way of life *so* hard. Separated lives, separated religions, this is what I *don't* want in my country.' Back at home, she thought, she would look with more determination for what she and others might do to try and stop the Dayton lines setting hard, cutting the ethnic groups of Bosnia adrift from each other once and for all. Seeing what the loss of co-existence means in Northern Ireland, 'Maybe', she thought, 'I'll become a stronger fighter.'

The Israeli visitors too were struck more than anything by the mistrust pervading Northern Ireland. It astonished them that even in the practised friendships of the Network there was hesitation about visiting each other's favoured places. The Network had organised a social for their Israeli guests in a pub. It was not too far from the city centre, a place they felt would be respectful and welcoming of a crowd of women - something you couldn't say of every drinking spot in the city. But this otherwise ideal spot was a well known Republican venue. Some of the Protestant women in the Network, including the Israelis' closest friends, felt uneasy about attending. In the end it was mainly the women from Catholic areas who turned up for the party with the Israelis.

The two Palestinian women, Nahla Shedafni and Rosette Abu Rahmon, talked a lot afterwards about this 'night of the Irish pub'. Nahla said,

> They aren't living together. They aren't understanding each other ... A lot of the women said 'We are not going to this place'. And I said 'You are Catholic women and Protestant women. You are our friends and we'll go each together. It's not a problem.' But they said 'No!' And I was just so surprised and sorry.

That this was not just a failure of friendship however, and that the Protestant women were not entirely paranoid, was borne out on a subsequent occasion when we did visit, as a mixed group, an identifiably Catholic pub in a Catholic village. Our Protestant colleague, recognised by her car number plates, was threateningly tailed home to her Protestant area by an unknown car. The threat in such circumstances can come even-handedly from 'the enemy' and from those policing loyalty to one's 'own' side. Either way, it is trouble you try to avoid.

The Jewish women in the visiting group, Lily Traubmann and Vera Jordan, also felt shaken by such pervasive threats and fears in what seemed to them a relatively well-advanced peace process. If it could be like this here almost four hundred years after the settlers took the land, it depressingly seemed to push the possibilities of peaceful co-existence in Israel/Palestine, where settlement continues by the hour, over the horizon of a far distant future.

It is not surprising that, in these contrasted wars, with their dissimilar peace processes and varying constructions of ethno-national identity, the Network, Medica and Bat Shalom did not have exactly the same approach to what the Belfast women call 'making democracy out of difference'. The Network found itself challenging Medica to be more explicit about 'identity', but being challenged on the same ground by Bat Shalom.

In the Women's Support Network, they have really struggled towards an important understanding: that we cannot just skate over the hurt we do each other in the name of politicised identities. Marie Mulholland, who was the co-ordinator of the Women's Support Network at the time of the exchange visits, told the Medica women,

> I don't think it's always safe to assume we all think the same way about everything. Because our different experiences and different backgrounds give us different perceptions on things. And sometimes we've found that out quite painfully. And that we have to have a way in our own organisations to have a safe space where we can talk about stuff that's painful.

Talking to the Bosnian women, the Belfast four felt worried by what they felt was a sort of silence on ethnic identity in Medica. They understood that Bosnian people want to put the war behind them, that they would like to jump clean back to the days when ethnic difference had not counted for much. But Gillian wondered - could Bosnia be thought to be *so* different from Northern Ireland?

Talking with Selena about this, she recalled,

> When I first joined the Network I felt different. But I never discussed it, never talked about it and never really felt part of the Network because at that stage I would have felt the dominant culture within the Network was Catholic and Republicanism and I as a Protestant did not feel there was a place there for my opinions, my beliefs. And I know other Protestants felt the same but they didn't discuss it because it didn't seem appropriate, or there wasn't space to express how we felt. Could it be that women in Medica are meeting together and you assume they feel OK but some might feel silenced by the fact that they're different?

Selena agreed - it was possible that Bosnian Serb or Bosnian Croat might feel this way in predominantly Muslim areas like Zenica today. And later, the N. Ireland visitors made friends with a Croatian woman in the town who told them in no uncertain words that in this post-war period the nationalist Muslim party controlling the government are fostering a society that privileges Muslims and discriminates against Croats and other 'others'.

Talking in greater depth to women in Medica, it was clear that Rada, of Bosnian Serb background, felt ambivalent about the lack of emphasis on ethnic difference within the project. On the one hand, yes, everyone wants to forget all that ethnic-speak. It was the source of nothing but trouble. But on the other hand each of them, Bosnian Serb, Bosnian Croat, Bosnian Muslim, all democrats though they may be, has a different kind of pain about the things that happened, different kinds of loss. Rada's Bosnian Serb parents had been killed by a Bosnian Serb shell. As a Bosnian Serb, she has been forcibly labelled by an insurgent Serb nationalism with a 'name' she never did much identify with and which now, to make matters worse, is one of the most reviled identities in the world. Does she not make sense of such an event from a unique situatedness? For a Bosnian Muslim the recent changes mean something different. She might perhaps have preferred to remain a Yugoslav than to become a Bosnjak. But at  least there is something in Muslim identity today to be cling to: survivor pride.

Perhaps, in the interests of making the alliance within Medica real and durable, it would be helpful to acknowledge differences like this. Gillian said,

> You can see there's huge gaping wounds here. And you know that reconciliation is quite difficult. But people keep referring here to 'we were mixed before the war and we're still mixed'. But that isn't reconciliation. That's like there's been a gap. The war's happened. The most bloody bitter thing that could happen to people. And it hasn't been talked about … And the next thought is, I would have said to you - it's almost as if there's a denial there. Or maybe it's because the pain's so deep.

The fact is, though, that political boundaries in the two countries are differently structured. In Belfast you come up against one every time you want to go from the supermarket to the swimming pool. In Zenica there is no Belfast-style territoriality. The segregation lines are far away. They are the Dayton lines that divide the Muslim-Croat Federation from the Serb Entity, and the lines of separation that Croat extremists try to draw round territories they claim. So, segregation, reconciliation and unification of Bosnia can seem like something only politicians can influence.

Ethnic identities get too easily picked up and used by outsiders who take nationalist discourse at face value. International agencies and NGOs try to foster reconciliation between named 'sides'. But both the Bosnians and the Northern Ireland women had sometimes felt manipulated by them. Selena said, 'There are attempts from groups where there are Muslims working with those parts in Bosnia where there are mainly Serbs living, and vice versa. But it's not coming from the heart, wanting to get to know each other, but to fit funding criteria.' This made the Belfast women laugh in recognition. Gillian said, 'We would have had a long history of funders telling us that Protestants and Catholics should meet, and when we fill in the forms we have to have the same number of Protestants meeting the same number of Catholics.'

It is this kind of thing that makes the women of both Medica and the Women's Support Network reluctant to stress ethnicity. And the gap between the Network and Medica on this anyway seemed to become narrower in the

light of the greater differences between the Network and Bat Shalom. The Bat Shalom women can never be in doubt for a moment who among them, or in their environment, is 'Jewish' and who is 'Palestinian'. They live in contrasted environments, have different kinds of jobs, sometimes dress distinctively, have a different relationship to Hebrew and Arabic languages. Also, it is their style to be outspoken with each other and never hesitate to 'name names'. The women of the Women's Support Network, when visiting Bat Shalom, were sometimes startled by their roughness with each other.

By contrast the Network women are adept at 'being appropriate'. They avoid using the terms Catholic and Protestant, which they feel are inaccurate and often abused both by ignorant onlookers and motivated parties to the conflict. Instead they talk about 'tradition', 'background' or 'community', or the area you live in or come from. They talk about beliefs rather than belonging: nationalist and Republican politics and unionist or Loyalist convictions.

The trouble is that outsiders coming to Belfast cannot tell by looking or listening who is who. They do not know the codes, euphemisms and synonyms in the Northern Ireland political thesaurus. Because of the tactful reticence, the inexplicitness, of the Network women, the Israeli women sometimes felt at sea, driving through Portadown, visiting a community project in South Armagh or having a guided tour round a former gaol that had housed political prisoners. *Which side were they on?* 'Why did you not tell us' Vera asked the Network women later, 'whether the groups we were visiting, or the women we were meeting, were Catholic or Protestant?' The exemplary 'non-closure' on ethno-political identity, learned by the Belfast women to avoid the destructive stereotyping that is so prevalent in their political environment, sometimes seemed to the Bat  Shalom women like a coyness, an evasion of difference running contrary to the Network's founding principle of 'affirming difference'.

So the programme of exchange visits was an exercise in two-level transversal politics. Groups already organising transversally across internal ethno-political fault lines stepped laterally across state borders into strange places where they found themselves responding to marked differences of culture and divergent historical trajectories. The exercise was riven with contradictions, uncertainties and risks.

First, accurate and deep communication of meanings across wide differences of experience is not easy to achieve or sustain at the best of times. And in this case there was a serious language problem. We employed interpreters for particular moments of the trips, including the workshops and seminars. But the project lacked funding for continuous interpretation facilities, so that for much of the time women had to depend on their own and each other's language skills. Besides, much of the pleasure lay in the informal moments of friendship, outside the working day, when an interpreter, even had she been a possibility, would have been an intrusion.

Second, in comparison with a carefully facilitated preliminary meeting between the three projects we had held a couple of years before, the process was wildly uncontrolled. At the earlier workshop, held in Spain, it had been in our power to take great pains to ensure that each participant quickly felt herself to be recognised and heard. We had been able to pick up on distress as soon as it surfaced. The negotiation of self-presentations by the groups had been painstaking. By contrast, on these exchange trips the participants were scattered about, living in the homes of different hosts. The organisational emphasis was on practical logistics of travel, visits, entertainment. Nobody was responsible for feelings. At times it was a rough ride.

One way in which we sometimes seemed to be on a roller-coaster was in the nature of the emotionally-loaded material we were continually addressing. The projects all sustain their alliances in turbulent environments by consciously or semi-consciously restricting the agenda of matters on which they normally work together. Of course the agenda must always have enough of substance on it to make the alliance concrete and worthwhile. But at the same time certain matters, too divisive to be safely handled, must be tacitly relegated to that zone of 'any other business' that we rarely get around to.

In the encounter between projects, these conventions were inevitably breached. The newcomers would ask innocent questions, questions that in their own project they felt confident to address but which could catch their respondents unprepared. Besides, they were going on visits to quite other projects in the host areas, visiting groups that were not cross-community alliances but situated outspokenly on one side or other of the line of national conflict. All of this could put stress on the internal cohesion of the projects.

There was consequently an interesting dynamic going on between the two levels of transversalism. The four women who travelled together in each direction, although nominally part of the same project, had not necessarily had occasion to know each other well at home before the journey. The trip threw them into unaccustomed proximity. Often they were sharing a bedroom. They could sometimes look misleadingly like an unproblematic unity, rather than what they were: differentiated individuals who perhaps disagreed with each other, felt unsure with each other. They sometimes had to speak in public, for the group, without being able to consult each other first. It was sometimes difficult to be true to one's own sense of self without upsetting and alienating colleagues by choice of words, choice of emphasis. It has to be said however that retrospectively most of the travellers noted 'getting to know women of my own project better' as having been a valuable by-product of the journey. Responding to questions from outsiders about their relationships to each other had made them analyse them more closely and value them more consciously.

It was difficult to ensure that the benefits of the experience to the travelling four accrued to their projects as a whole. Feedback is complicated. Just as you need good storytelling skills to get your reality across to those other projects you visit, so you need them to recount these political travels meaningfully to those at home. We hoped the videos might help. But these, inevitably, were about the journey of the eye behind the camera and the voice behind the script, which were mine, not theirs. And language comes into it again: how to translate the scripts from English into local languages for showing in Medica and Bat Shalom?

A final uncertainty concerns the framing of these exchanges in a context of research. At times it had been annoying to be watched, questioned or filmed. It risked spoiling the intimate moments, blurring the immediacy of the experience. But a gain may have been greater reflexivity. There was someone continually asking questions, wondering about what was going on. And a lot of writing is being done about the exercise in the hope of generating a wide discussion about the doing of transversal politics. Everything I write is shown to the women involved before it goes to press. They are usually generous in insisting only on changes to words that are intolerable, letting pass the milder discomfort that comes of being talked about, the misfit of someone else's analysis, someone else's terminology. But, just as the videos recorded what my eyes chose to see, so the articles are, in the end, a researcher's view.

A bove all, though, discomfort came from the fact that the researcher chose to focus not on the actual day to day product, the output, of the projects but on the feature of difference. Partly, a cross-community alliance works because you keep your eyes on the road, on the job you are meant to be doing: fund-raising, administering, giving therapy, issuing a press release. That I continually asked for a discussion of identity processes, ethno-political differentiation and internal democracy was annoying to the projects at times. I felt I was using, mostly necessarily but sometimes crassly, terms they spend their lives avoiding, deconstructing and nuancing: Catholic, Protestant, Serb, Croat, Muslim, Arab, Jew. In stressing one kind of difference, I was always in danger of submerging others. In particular there was a risk of losing sight of the important differences within major collectivities - the many kinds of Bosnian Muslim, let's say, the extraordinary complexity that variants of secularism, religion, urban or rural culture, relationship to the former Yugoslav state, confer on contemporary Bosnia. Above all, the fact that I wished the visiting groups to fairly represent the majorly conflictual ethno-national groups in the project - that I was asking, please, for two 'Catholics' and two 'Protestants' - was running counter to anti-'naming' practice in the projects. It was going beyond 'affirming difference' to the point of reifying it. But how else, I asked myself, to get them to articulate their discomfort with this and to spell out the intelligent, useful, sideways steps they choose instead? How else can I tell it if I don't hear them say it?

The exchange programme between Medica, the Women's Support Network and Bat Shalom was, I think, on balance useful. They are just now in the process of evaluating it themselves. No significant damage was done. There may have been significant gains. It seems that Medica and the Network may continue to work together, the Bosnians bringing trauma counselling skills to Belfast, the Northern Ireland women taking community development know-how to Zenica.

But if the trans-national learning was viable, it was because of two qualities the projects brought to it. First, it was important that each of the three had the experience of being a difficult alliance. It saved them from falling too heavily onto one side or the other on the conflictual terrain they visited. It enabled them, instead of simply 'condemning the oppressor' and questioning the propriety of co-operation, to value and endorse the commitment of the host group to negotiating democracy in a situation deformed by injustice. Second, the intrinsic robustness of the projects, the strength and flexibility of their internal relationships, enabled them to thrive and grow on the new material they found themselves working on. Instead, as might have happened, of being destabilised and divided by the challenge. Less experienced transversalists, less skilled at translations, might have fared worse.

# Difficult alliances
## *Treading the minefield of identity and solidarity politics*
## Pragna Patel

Pragna Patel *discusses the work of Southall
Black Sisters.*

Southall Black Sisters (SBS) is a collective of South Asian women.[1] We operate an advice, resource and campaigning centre for women in Southall, an area in west London with a large South Asian population. In comparison with many other Asian communities in this country, Southall is heterogeneous and has a cosmopolitan feel to it. All religions and ethnic groups of the Indian Subcontinent are present there, although the Punjabi Sikh ethnic group and religion are dominant.

In the last decade or so Southall has also received a large influx of Somalian refugees, of predominantly Muslim background, who are now beginning to establish themselves as a cultural and social force in the area. They have already changed the social landscape of the area but have not, as yet, asserted a strong political presence. It remains to be seen when and how Somalian women, who are at present pre-occupied with addressing language, housing and educational needs, will assert themselves. At present they remain largely invisible in the public religious and cultural spaces created by Somalian men.

---

1. This article is based on my own perception of the daily work of Southall Black Sisters and the concerns that arise from it. It does not necessarily reflect the views of SBS as an organisation.

The Southall Black Sisters centre caters for all women. We operate an open door policy, providing a front line service for all women irrespective of ethnic and religious background. The focus of much of our work, however, reflecting the make-up of the local population, is on South Asian women. Over the years, our campaigning and political work has been largely dictated by the issues and concerns raised in the casework that we undertake. It is the experiences of women who use the centre, combined with our own, that have shaped our progressive feminist outlook.

The centre was set up in 1983 with funding from the local council. We continue to rely on funds from a variety of sources to provide much needed emergency and longterm casework services for black women. The very existence of the centre reflects the fact that the needs of black[2] and minority women are not adequately addressed either by indigenous institutions within the community or by the wider state institutions. The bulk of the casework undertaken at the centre has to do with domestic and sexual violence. This means we also find ourselves addressing the attendant problems of forced arranged marriages, abductions of children and young girls, homelessness and poverty. The other side of the coin is that we are also obliged to scrutinise the state's responses, including the response of the police, to these issues.

## Identities and alliances

Our practice at SBS has shown us that identity and alliance building are closely connected. In fact we would look on them as twin concepts. We must be involved in alliance-building if our aim is to work towards a more egalitarian society. And the identities we choose can either limit or increase the potential for the alliance-building.

In a sense, the history of SBS can be seen as a history of resisting imposed identities. We have, throughout our twenty year history, attempted to shake off identities foisted on us by the community, the anti-racist movement and the state. Reactionary elements within our communities seek to impose identities on us through the confining of women to their traditional roles as wives and

2. The term 'black' was adopted at the inception of SBS as a political label, to reflect the common processes of colonialism and racism experienced by women of Asian and African-Caribbean origins. It has served a useful mobilising or alliance-building function.

mothers, with the aim of ensuring that cultural and religious values remain intact and are transmitted from one generation to the next. We have also had to resist attempts by the more progressive anti-racist movements to pin a singular black identity on us. Such constructions, sometimes overtly but more often tacitly, demand subjugation of all other identities for the greater good of racial justice. (I discuss this further with Marie Mulholland in 'Inclusive Movements/ Movements for Inclusion' (p127). This has led to a denial of other experiences and identities such as those arising from gender, caste, class and other divisions within our communities. In addition to this, we have found ourselves having to resist racist stereotypes and categories fostered by the British state, the effect of which has been to subordinate difference, denigrate minority cultures and religions, and confine us to the status of second class (or, as in the case of refugees, third class) citizens.

More recently, we have been engaged in resisting very specific fundamentalist and nationalist identities that have been fostered by the rise of Sikh, Muslim and Hindu religious fundamentalist/nationalist movements in this country and abroad. The reformulations of identity being imposed in these processes have direct political consequences for progressive, democratic, anti-racist struggles and for women's demands for self-determination. These movements demand absolute conformity to religious laws as interpreted by male religious leaders, in denial of countless variations in interpretation of religious/cultural practices that have evolved within different black and minority communities.

Our experience as black and minority women in Britain shows that constructions of identity are constantly in a state of flux. They are for ever being negotiated and re-negotiated in social and political processes, here and abroad. For example, on the one hand, the construction of fundamentalist religious identities within minority communities in the UK has been a response to British state racism and events in countries of origin. On the other hand, such constructions have been underpinned by conservative imperatives to maintain 'authentic' cultural and religious values perceived to be under threat in the West. Religious fundamentalist leaders have been able to utilise the new-found religious identities to gain power and control over local territories, communities and resources.

But above all, the history of SBS has been about the juggling of different identities. We have understood that we all carry with us a multiplicity of identities, reflecting the numerous struggles that we are simultaneously engaged in - struggles against racial and class inequality, against patriarchal oppression and religious fundamentalism. We have not been able to give primacy to any one identity, because to do so would have amounted to hiding other realities and signalling the view that our struggles can be hierarchically ordered. On the other hand we have found it important to recognise that at certain moments some struggles do become more urgent than others, with the effect that some aspects of our identities momentarily take on more significance.

The beginning of SBS, as an organisation comprising African-Caribbean and Asian women, is instructive. It was in a sense, a first break with the labels imposed on us by others. It was also an important moment in the history of collaboration between African-Caribbean and Asian feminists. The forming of SBS involved the forging of a new feminist secular identity, one based on a shared history of racism, and of religious and patriarchal control. The absence of the recognition of gender power relations within anti-racist movements and the absence of an acknowledgement of racism within white feminist movements had resulted in the invisibility of black and minority women. This invisibility is what gave rise to the need for an organisation like SBS, and it remains a major hurdle to be overcome.

A conscious decision was taken to set up as an autonomous black women's group. We did not wish to separate ourselves off from anti-racist and other progressive movements, but there was a need to create space in which women's experiences could be shared and articulated. From the start there was an emphasis on the commonality of our experiences and the need to work out a common agenda for change. This stress on shared experiences and the need for an inclusive approach in our thinking and practice was what guided us out of the paralysis that was gripping many other women's groups. As an early member of SBS put it, 'We made a conscious decision to move beyond slogans and develop solidarity on the basis of mutual understanding of both the similarities and differences in our experiences as Asian and Afro-Caribbean women and then to translate this understanding into practice. None of this was easy'. It was not easy then, but the task of sustaining alliances across difference has become even more difficult since.

The hard fact is that we have failed to sustain Asian and African-Caribbean unity within SBS. Practically, politically and theoretically we have maintained a commitment to such unity. But the local population in which we are situated is largely Asian, with the effect that the activities and campaigns of the organisation are mainly geared to meeting the needs of Asian women. Our alliance also floundered because (although we have learnt the lesson now) in the past we simply translated unity into practice by operating a 'quota system'. For example, we made the decision to ensure that, funding permitting, the number of Asian and African-Caribbean workers

'the task of sustaining alliances across difference has become even more difficult'

in the project would be equal, regardless of the needs of the women coming to the centre. The need to be visibly an alliance took precedence over the need to realistically ensure a more effective and long-term alliance.

Sustaining an African-Caribbean and Asian alliance in SBS has also been difficult because the priorities of the communities differ, partly a reflection of the different ways racism is experienced. For example we have witnessed the break up of Caribbean families, whereas extended families within Asian communities have been bolstered. But both sets of experiences have come about as a result of the centrality given to 'multiculturalism' in British politics - something I return to below. This state strategy has had profound consequences for the roles that Asian and Caribbean women occupy within the family, leading to differing priorities in terms of immediate action. For example Asian women have been active around domestic violence and other forms of restriction within the family, whereas many African Caribbean women have been active around educational under-achievement and the problem of expulsions of their children from schools.

## Relations with community and state

Over the years in Southall Black Sisters we have learned to develop an understanding of how constructions of 'race', gender and class intersect to lock black and minority women in subordinate positions of powerlessness in the home and outside. Demands for freedom and for more choices for women has meant challenging and negotiating with powerful conservative forces within our communities and at the same time challenging and negotiating with the racist state. When we deal with domestic violence, for example, we are not simply dealing with a gender issue but simultaneously with the question of how the state responds to such violence and to demands from women for protection.

One of SBS's current campaigns has been around the so called 'one year rule' within immigration law, which stipulates that people coming to the UK to join their spouse must remain in the marriage for at least one year before they can apply to stay permanently. The operation of this rule means that women whose immigration status is dependent on that of their husband cannot afford to appeal to the state for protection in the case of domestic violence. The effect is that the meagre but nevertheless real choices available to women in the majority community are not available to women with an unsettled immigration status. The rule effectively operates to perpetuate patriarchal oppression for women experiencing violence. So SBS campaigns for the abolition of the 'one year rule' and its attendant provisions, arguing that women should be able to avail themselves of the legal and welfare resources they need in order to live free from the violence, but without fear of deportation.

Immigration law also has an alternative effect. A series of immigration laws have been enacted by successive Tory and Labour governments designed quite clearly to keep out black (that is third world) men, in particular from the Indian Subcontinent. Sometimes therefore a woman will come to SBS having experienced violence from a man whose right to reside in the UK is dependent on his marriage to her. If the marriage breaks down in such a case it is the man who is liable to deportation. Sometimes such a woman understandably asks us, for her protection, to support her in having her violent husband deported.

However to accede to this request would be to legitimate both racist immigration rules and practices and the state brutality that often accompanies their implementation. Many of us remember the recent case of Joy Gardner who met her death when she tried to resist police and immigration officers arresting her for deportation to Jamaica. Instead SBS has tried to develop a practice that is simultaneously anti-racist and anti-sexist. For example, in the scenario just outlined, our first priority would be to help the woman seek protection from the criminal and civil justice systems and if necessary refer her to a safe house or refuge. But using deportation as a means of protection is something we feel we cannot entertain.

Racism and racial violence can be experienced in different (gendered) ways by women. One classic example, although it has not, to our knowledge, been repeated since, is the virginity tests carried out on Asian women at Heathrow airport in the late 1970s. Immigration officers devised this physical test as a means of sifting out *'bona fide'* from 'bogus' women who, they asserted, were fraudulently posing as fiancées to evade immigration restrictions and gain entry to this country.

The state's adoption of a policy known as 'multiculturalism', especially within the legal and social welfare system, has been particularly damaging for women. Multiculturalism replaces a former, less articulated, policy of 'integration' and is currently the state's chosen means for mediating relations between itself and minority communities. It presents a progressive face, in recognising the desire of people of minority cultures in the UK to retain a distinct identity rather than having it submerged in the dominant culture. At best, it seems to promise a tolerance of heterogeneity.

The problem with multiculturalism however is that it conceptualises minority communities as homogeneous entities with no internal divisions. Gender, class, and caste differences are obscured. It involves the state in a subtle but pervasive way in intervening to construct identities, with racist and anti-democratic effects. Such homogenising constructions of minority communities are born out of the state's endorsement of community leaders. These leaders are un-elected, usually religious and often conservative males, with little if any interest in social justice and equality. Yet they claim to be the 'authentic' spokespersons for the community and are the main power-brokers, regularly consulted (usually informally) by the police and other state institutions. This multiculturalist contract between state and community leaders amounts to the former granting the latter a degree of communal autonomy (usually over the family and women) in return for acquiescence and preservation of the status quo.

We have witnessed devastating effects of multicultural policies in the everyday lives of women. They reinforce authoritarian, undemocratic, patriarchal institutions and relations within the community. Multiculturalism has been utilised to great effect by fundamentalist forces seeking to control women's sexuality and prevent alliances and progressive movements from being built.

## Creating secular spaces

Within SBS, maintaining alliances amongst ourselves as South Asian women has not been difficult because of the centrality given to the term secularism. This is not for us an abstract or merely theoretical term. It is actually put into practise in creating a space of mutual respect amongst women. Our starting point is that whether a woman wishes to interpret and practise religion, or to reject religion and culture in part or altogether, her choice is equally legitimate. Our constitution enshrines anti-communal, anti-racist, feminist, secular and egalitarian principles. It has not been difficult to put this into practice because women readily understand the commonality of their experiences as women. Many of the users of the centre are only too aware that as women from the Indian Subcontinent they share one cultural patchwork quilt, criss-crossed though it is by different religions. Language, food, films, as well as such heavy duty concepts as shame and honour, are just some of the shared ingredients that go towards making up the social fabric of their lives. For example, in debates about domestic violence or religious oppression, women are readily able to identify with each other's predicament. They negotiate their differences and arrive at a common stance against domestic violence in solidarity with each other.

By contrast, within the official language of multiculturalism, differences amongst South Asians have been distorted and exaggerated. It is of course important to recognise new variants of racism affecting relations between minority communities - including the disturbing rise of Islamophobia. But many of the differences that are being emphasised are absurd and exaggerated. And they have serious implications. They can affect the ability of projects to obtain funding. And they are politically damaging in that they limit the possibility of alliances between different Asian women. For example, a recent Home Office research on the needs of Pakistani Muslim women in the face of domestic violence, highlighted the problems of the 'one year rule' (mentioned above) and the concept of *izzat*, or honour, as if these were exclusive to Muslim women. There was nothing in the experiences cited by the research that could in fact be singled out as being exclusively 'Muslim'. Yet the signs are that social policy is heading towards this kind of spurious recognition of difference, which merely serves to legitimate the creation of new (fragmented) categories of Sikhs, Muslims, Hindus.

We find that the women who come to the SBS centre themselves defy imposed identities and labels that serve to separate them from each other. In a recent wave of Sikh and Muslim fundamentalist rivalry and violent activity in Southall, the women at SBS recognised immediately the dangers this represented to their autonomy and freedom, and to community peace. They insisted on organising a women's march through a main street in Southall. They wanted to reclaim the community for themselves, to stop what was being done in their name as Sikh, Hindu and Muslims and to assert their right to be recognised as equal citizens of the community. Their actions in effect served to redefine the notion of community.

Because our starting point is to develop a secular and anti-communal organisation, we have been able to avoid some of the dilemmas that have beset other Asian women's groups in recent times. In some groups the transformation of identities from an inclusive Asian identity to exclusive religious ones has given rise to very real problems. For example, in one Asian women's group in East London, Muslim women made demands for a separate space within the centre, in which to meet as Muslim women only. They did not make this demand because they faced discrimination and exclusion as a minority within the centre, but because their religious identity, formulated in opposition to 'others', would not allow them to seek out common and shared experiences as Asian women living in a racist society. This kind of dilemma is not easily resolved. But it does point towards the need to create a secular feminist space which can guarantee religious tolerance and diversity, allowing for constant negotiation as to the use of the space for all women, without fear of being straitjacketed into fixed identities.

Injecting a personal note here, I must admit that the fragility of our alliances within SBS was brought home to me with the rise of Hindu nationalism and fundamentalism in India. I am of Hindu background, but had actually thought I had erased this in my quest to forge a black, progressive and feminist identity for myself. But as more virulent nationalist reconstructions of Hindu identity took hold, both in India and in Hindu communities in this country, I found myself forced to acknowledge that part of my identity. This was not because of the need to return to religion, but in opposition to the appalling hate crime - killings, rape, looting and burning of homes - being committed against Muslims in India. I had to take responsibility for what was being done in my name. But the Hinduism I now found I had to assert as part of a wider resistance movement was like that espoused by Mahatma Gandhi, more tolerant, humane and respectful of other religions.

The need to recognise my own Hindu background was forced on me at the conclusion of meeting organised by SBS in opposition to Hindu fundamentalism. A Muslim colleague broke down and wept at the end of the meeting because she felt as if she had been 'stripped of her humanity' by the language of hatred and violence espoused by certain rabid Hindu fundamentalists who had attended our meeting.

For the first time I was forced to recognise that, whilst I was part of a minority in this country, I was, at the same time, by virtue of my membership of the Hindu diaspora, part of the Hindu majority in India. Words fail you when you find yourself on opposite sides of a dividing line, separated from those with whom in the past you have fought side by side against all types of injustices. I could find no comforting words to utter. But the silence between us also helped us both to remember that we had, both of us, committed ourselves to maintaining at all cost, a secular anti-fundamentalist space within SBS. For me, hope lay in the fact that we had together resisted all forms of racism, religious fundamentalist and right wing movements and that this common stance might save us now from turning into enemies.

## Co-operation and alliance

There is a further problem in the relationships we need to build within our communities. We are forced to recognise that from time to time we need to seek and obtain the support of those who hold power within the community. And here perhaps we should make a clear distinction between the seeking of co-operation and the building of alliances.

SBS has recently had experience of working with Muslim organisations, including Muslim fundamentalist organisations, in our campaign to free Zoora Shah. Zoora Shah is a Pakistani Muslim woman who killed her male abuser after years of experiencing sexual abuse and economic exploitation. She was jailed for life in 1993, and SBS has initiated a campaign to free her and to expose the criminal justice system for its failure to understand the contexts in which abused women kill. In this complex case we have felt we have no choice but to seek the support of religious leaders. The reality is that the state is more likely to heed the demands of Muslim community leaders than those of a feminist group such as ourselves. It is one more concrete example of how multicultural politics works to the detriment of women within minority communities. It highlights the limits of our power, even when organised collectively as women.

We have of course had to adopt a different language in order to obtain the support of a wide range of Muslim organisations. We have found ourselves taking on a language of human rights and humanity, in place of our accustomed feminist language of autonomy and choice.

The response of these leaders to our request for support for Zoora Shah has been interesting. Out of some 600 Muslim organisations, including mosques, that we have contacted, only a bare handful have given total, unqualified support. Most Muslim leaders, ranging from fundamentalists to those who would view themselves as moderate liberals, have been silent or have refused to support the campaign. One reason is that, among fundamentalists and liberals alike, to be seen to support Zoora Shah is tantamount to acknowledging the patriarchal power relations that exist within our communities. Recognising such a thing would upset their goal: to get *sharia* law, or variations of it, introduced as an alternative to the present civil law in the UK, as a means of controlling Muslim women.

Yet more interesting has been the response of some Muslim organisations that have supported Zoora Shah, not on the basis that she is a woman who has the right to defend herself against male violence, but on a different basis: the need to oppose the British state as racist. According to them, Zoora Shah's exceedingly lengthy prison sentence is a manifestation of the state's 'barbaric' discrimination against her as a Muslim woman. Yet these same Muslim organisations have also unequivocally stated that if Zoora Shah lived in an Islamic state, subject to *sharia* laws, the proper punishment for her crime would be death. They argue that strict adherence to the Koran would find her as sinning because she has killed, and, furthermore, as sinning because she did not take steps to end the abuse. This, regardless of the fact that there are many obstacles, including those placed by religious and community leaders, preventing women like Zoora Shah from escaping male violence.

The chilling nature of this response aside, it is curious to note that one reason sometimes given for tempering *sharia* justice is that 'we are British Muslims' and will abide by the laws of this country. This assertion of 'Britishness' is bewildering, given the fact that Islamic revivalism in this country has fostered a Muslim identity precisely in opposition to the British state and to the 'West' in general. It is also ironical that this 'Britishness' extends to Muslim women only insofar as they conform to religious law. Any attempts by Muslim women to assert their 'Britishness' by for example determining their own sexuality, would be met with severe punishment for being a 'western' practice.

The support we have had from some Muslim organisations should not deflect attention from the underlying patriarchal, and even misogynist, trends within all religious fundamentalist movements. What the case illustrates is the complex ways in which newly formed religious identities have become enmeshed with anti-racist ones, and also how fundamentalists sometimes use the language of anti-racism to wield power and control within our communities.

The trouble is that, if seeking the support and co-operation of community leaders has been problematic for SBS, so too has working, as anti-racists, with anti-racist organisations within our communities. With a few exceptions, anti-racist commentators and activists, in their attempts to build an alliance against racism, have either remained silent about the reactionary character of community authorities, or at worst actively courted reactionary constituencies. Needless to say, an alliance formed on such a basis has significant ramifications for our involvement in these wider anti-racist struggles. A 'broad church' approach to racism is needed. But to mobilise rather than challenge these reactionary religious identities is to render expendable the rights of the most vulnerable sections of our community.

I do not think any of us can afford to underestimate the limitations and weaknesses of the struggles we wage as individual organisations on the basis of our distinctive identities. Feminism is currently short on activism and seriously weakened by fragmentation. Most of us would be hard pressed to draw a hundred people to our campaigns and events. There is no doubt that a practice of alliances is a precondition of a social movement for equality, justice and civil rights. The challenge is to find the terms on which such a movement can be genuinely inclusive.

# Inclusive movements/ movements for inclusion

## Marie Mulholland and Pragna Patel

*Transversal politics is an attempt to step back from a universalism that denies the significance of differentiating experiences, but at the same time to step beyond the fragmentation and rivalry of 'identity politics'.*

*We have seen this kind of careful footwork inside the Women's Support Network, Bat Shalom and Medica, and in their collaboration in the shared project called Women Building Bridges (See 'Crossing Borders', p99) We have also seen it at work inside Southall Black Sisters (See 'Difficult Alliances', p115).*

*But none of those projects is an alliance for the mere purpose of allying. Each exists to have an impact on a bigger system. Marie Mulholland and Pragna Patel discussed with Cynthia Cockburn the outward political moves of the Women's Support Network and Southall Black Sisters. Both projects have chosen to operate in wider coalitions that are incipient social movements against exclusion, inequality, injustice and violence.*

But, being women's projects, they also have to struggle within these movements, too often formed around a singular identity, to get them to take on those values as practices, not merely as demands.

**Cynthia** It seems to me that both the Women's Support Network and Southall Black Sisters put energy into two things: providing practical support for women, and acting as political subjects on a wider stage. They're about mobilising resources for service provision and mobilising coalitions around campaigns. What's the relationship between those two things?

**Marie** The Network came into being in response to an unfair decision by Belfast City Council. They refused funding to one of the women's centres, using sectarian arguments. Sectarianism (as well as some serious sexism and misogyny) was the kind of environment in which that decision was made. And so in challenging their decision, we knew we weren't like any other group. We weren't coming together simply to get resources, we were actually coming together to challenge the status quo on this one. So therefore that challenge had to be built in to who we were, how we formulated ourselves. There was that real sense in the original core group that came together that these were the things we could agree on. We were going to challenge discrimination wherever it occurs, and what we were going to replace it with was equality and justice. They were our common values, very clearly articulated. The trouble is, I think, the organisation has grown, and more and more groups have come into it, and now we're ten years old, and sometimes we forget to reiterate those principles for new people coming on board.

**Pragna** One of the things we grapple with all the time is that the political landscape has changed so much, so there are very few projects now that are political in any sense, and many more that are service provision projects. New people are coming in who don't really buy into the kind of political vision that those of us had when we started those projects. Is that what we're talking about here?

**Marie** Yes. But actually in Northern Ireland, a lot of the work that needs to go on, that I hope sometimes that we do contribute to, is constantly redefining what *is* political.

**Pragna** Exactly.

**Marie** And to get women comfortable with that, because politics with a capital P has always been something that working-class women in Northern Ireland have, if not rejected, certainly tried to avoid. They see it as divisive, as extremely male and one-dimensional in its focus. So for example we have a project called 'Women into Politics', which is about helping women define what they regard as political. To help them feel confident and comfortable and supported in being more up front about being political in their work and in their thinking. So, while we've been lobbying for resources for invisible and marginalised women, we've also had these more political projects that go on in parallel, in tandem with the everyday work. I think maybe we ought to look again at how do we integrate the two. The thing is, it implies two different relationships we have to have with the state. One is to see the state as a benign provider of resources, and hopefully we can access it, get what we need from it just for our services to function. The other is about challenging the state, which is I think what those political projects are about. So it's like the right hand is saying, 'It would be really nice if you'd give us some support', but the left hand hand is held out for structural change.

**Pragna** But I'm very conscious at Southall Black Sisters we wouldn't begin to be able to argue for change if we couldn't see what the needs were, where the state was failing to provide. In that sense the service provision goes hand in hand with the more political work. I think fundamentalist movements and right wing fascist movements have understood very well how to address the needs of ordinary men and women. That's why they have the popular appeal that left movements haven't often had. So I think that the service provision element in what we do is essential. And when you talk about the problem of integration between the two, I'm not sure that it's really that difficult. Because what we're saying to the state is basically: at best you can be a benign provider, and we challenge you because you *haven't* provided, and because you've constructed certain people as being outside the scope of your provision.

**Marie** I agree with that. Where I see the difficulty is in terms of the impact with the women involved in the organisation - if they don't see both things together, how are they going to get the political principles behind the organisation? And I think it is possible at this stage in our development for women to come into the organisation and take a route through it which means they never have to come into contact with the political at that intense level of political organisation.

**Cynthia** Does this challenge to the state depend on you being operational alliances? Could it be done by, say, a Catholic women's project, or a Protestant women's project, or one that was Hindu, Muslim or Sikh women acting alone?

**Pragna** For me I think the alliance is necessary because a hundred voices are going to be heard more than a single voice. I think that the need for alliances works at these two levels. One, it's about being heard by the state. But also it's about listening to each other. Alliance is necessary because it's too easy to remain in some sort of ghettoised politics. It's very easy to do what the state does, which is to elevate your experience somehow, so that you see yourself as the only group that suffers. It puts you into competition with each other, and allows the state to demonise others, to exclude others. So if you're talking about inclusion as being part of the new democratic order you're arguing for, then you've got to start talking to your neighbours, I think.

**Marie** The other motivation for that kind of coalition in alliance building is also to try and provide another way of people relating to each other than in hierarchies of oppression. Because that's what happens as well. And in some ways it's about creating some kind of level ground in which everybody can have some space together. It's about trying to get beyond or circumnavigate the kind of competitiveness of needs and agendas that goes on when people are marginalised. And also to get beyond the one-dimensional view of identity. I think that's really important and I think that oppression, one of the syndromes of oppression is that you become self-oppressed almost, and you only see yourself in fairly rigid terms. There's a rigidity about oppression that operates within the oppressed group, so you never get to see you can be more than what you are. And I think alliances do give a route through to talking about that. When we're successful, I think, we give women the possibility of being more than they presently are, in the sense of identity. I don't mean in the sense of their worth, although obviously we do tend to add to women's sense of their own value. But I mean all of us feel straitjacketed by these very narrow definitions of identity, and what I think we do together is try to give ourselves some more options around identity. A suit that you can grow into rather than a suit that narrows you.

**Pragna** Amazing! And there's another thing. I think it's very easy to look at the state and to look at power in a one-dimensional way. And alliances enable you to understand how power also works in different ways, horizontally as well as vertically. They help you understand better how power connects, how different kinds of power connect.

**Cynthia** By horizontally, do you mean being aware of the potential for oppression within the group?

**Pragna** Oppression within communities and in different sections of society. Simultaneously different types of power relationships at different levels are being played out, and you understand the connections better if you work in alliances. Because you have to acknowledge those positions of privilege or power that certain groups occupy, interrogate the way the state confers that privilege and power.

**Marie** I don't know whether privilege is quite the right word. But certainly it's about acknowledging that there are individuals within the collective who have experiences which give them routes and channels which maybe others don't have. I'm thinking for instance of Protestant women in the Network. They don't have any real power, because they're from working-class ghettos. And, what's more, because they're *women* from those ghettos. But maybe that part of their identity which is Loyalist will give them a route to people in their community who do have power. And it's about acknowledging that and using that to support the collective. So yes, I think the alliances we create sometimes help us to understand horizontal differences of power. I'm still not sure what effect we're having on the vertical power system.

**Cynthia** I remember that the Network was involved in a project called 'Making Women Seen and Heard'. That seemed to me both to use the means of horizontal alliance building and to address the vertical power system.

**Marie** That, I think, is the most productive and overtly political initiative we've undertaken. It was a project targeted at the most marginalised women across the whole of Northern Ireland and the border counties of the Republic. The backdrop was the peace process, which women didn't feel part of at all. They didn't feel that the process was constructed in a way that would allow them to contribute to it practically, and they wanted to. What could we do that would be practically of help to those women in challenging the processes behind their marginalisation?

And the thing is, there was a tool to hand. In fact we had the tool before we had the project. The tool was the PAFT Guidelines. PAFT stands for Policy Appraisal and Fair Treatment. It is a set of rules governing the public sector in Northern Ireland, and it doesn't apply in Britain. It requires equality of opportunity and treatment by redressing exclusion on the basis of religious belief, political opinion, gender, marital status, having or not having a dependent, ethnicity, disability, age and sexual orientation. Well, women are the most marginal of all those marginalised groups. We thought: if we could make PAFT known and understood, and teach women how to use it, that would empower them to challenge the inequality in decision-making that was marginalising them.

And we started by 'PAFTing' ourselves. We equality-proofed 'Making Women Seen and Heard'. We tried to make its structure a model of good practice. The most marginalised women were involved in decision-making, in deciding how resources would be allocated within the project. And rather than, say, me, an urban Catholic woman, going out into a rural Protestant area and trying to target women, we would have a rural Protestant woman on line within this project, who was part of the decision making, who could target those women herself. So it was 'like talking to like'. Then getting like to come into the room with women very unlike themselves. But they'd be women who had experienced another sort of discrimination and spoke a similar language of marginalisation.

We set it up on a geographical basis, so there were forums in six areas, each with various sectors of marginalised groups - disabled, carers and so on. We used the women in the project to organise the forums in their own locales, bringing the different sector groups together. There'd be maybe 70 women. And we'd deliver a kind of training programme, but it was actually more a two-way dialogue, asking them what they saw as the immediate causes of their marginalisation. In rural areas women were saying transport, they were saying child care, they were saying distance from the places where decisions are made. They were talking about rural poverty and the breakdown of rural infrastructure. Older women were talking about their isolation generally. Both Protestant and Catholic women were talking about their feeling of not being part of a political process. But there was one issue that was major, it was common to women right across the spectrum of oppression - and that was domestic violence. No matter where we went, no matter who was in the room, domestic violence kept coming up as an issue.

The idea was perhaps there'd be ten women out of any one forum who'd take on more intensive training, who'd become local empowerers of other women. So we'd always leave behind this activist layer, that was the idea. And they'd use PAFT for instance to challenge the mechanisms for allocating the European Peace Fund money. One group challenged the decision to close down a local maternity hospital. And 'Making Women Seen and Heard' was part of a wider movement for the implementation of fair treatment. We were saying something about the content of the peace process that was going on at the time.

**Pragna** There are two things you've said that make me think about Southall Black Sisters and how we've worked. One is that thing about domestic violence. One of the reasons we've been able to work so successfully across divides between Asian communities, even though they've been exacerbated by the rise of fundamentalisms, is precisely that we've focused on the issue of domestic violence. That wasn't a pre-determined agenda when the project was set up. We really had no idea what we were going to end up dealing with. We could easily have found ourselves specialising in employment issues, not domestic violence. But most of the women coming to us, regardless of their background, ethnic, religious or whatever, were coming to us because of domestic violence.

**Cynthia** Domestic violence is an issue with very different implications from employment, isn't it. Because if you're looking at domestic violence you're immediately focused not only on the state but also on the family and the community.

**Pragna** Yes. If we'd wanted to make our life easier we could have dealt with issues that are external to the community. But it wouldn't have shown up the contradictions as well as we've been able to do. That's happened exactly because working on domestic violence has meant interrogating the family and the community as well as the state.

**Marie** I think that domestic violence is a way of allowing women to come together because it's what they all have in common, no matter what they are, who they are, where they come from.

**Cynthia** In terms of experience - but does it readily translate immediately into a politics in which they're challenging big powers?

**Pragna** Well, yes and no. The interesting thing about domestic violence is you're on the one hand having to look at what goes on within the community, exposing the reactionary movements who'd like to keep a lid on domestic violence, exposing the patriarchal values of the community and family. And on the other hand, it's forcing you to engage with the state and make demands of the state. Challenging the community leaders and the state is about challenging big powers. Because women are saying 'we want protection from domestic violence'. That's where the state comes in. Who is doing the protecting? So we've found at Southall Black Sisters that the issue of domestic violence gives us an incredible insight into the way in which the state operates. I'm talking about the police, the legal system, the criminal justice system and so on. It's given us an insight into how the state colludes with leaders within the community to keep a lid on domestic violence, in ways that make it very difficult for women's needs to be met.

But the other thing I wanted to pick up on is this question of going beyond service provision to building social movements. Transversal politics it seems to me is about people being able to come together across differences, understanding where each other is coming from, understanding the different power relationships that exist, but at the same time being able to overcome those differences, however painful and difficult they are, in order, first, to sustain an alliance. But not only that. It's also so that the alliance can work to bring about some kind of wider transformation. And envisaging that wider transformation means subscribing to some kind of common agenda for change, from wherever you're positioned. And I'm thinking very much for example of the way in which say 'Women Against Fundamentalism' has functioned.

**Cynthia** 'Women Against Fundamentalism', it seems to me, was to Southall Black Sisters rather what 'Making Women Seen and Heard' was to the Women's Support Network, a kind of step outwards, a step into a social movement?

**Pragna** Yes. 'Women Against Fundamentalism'[1] is a group of women who came together from a number of different ethnic and religious backgrounds. It includes English women of Protestant background, Irish women of Catholic background, Jewish women, Asian women of various religious backgrounds, and so on. It's been one of the most thoughtful and effective alliances of black and white women we've ever been involved in. WAF's focus was very much on the ways in which the rise of religious fundamentalist movements has impacted on women, and the choice or lack of it they have in their lives as women. We are also explicitly anti-racist, not buying into those criticisms of fundamentalism that were anti-Muslim, for instance. Obviously given the composition of WAF there are horizontal differences among us in relation to power. But what's made it possible I think to deal with the internal differences and inequalities, is that we've looked first and foremost at the role the British state is playing in demonising certain minority communities. Addressing power, the state, has always been central to WAF's approach. And I can't overstate the impact that analysis had on SBS's practice and thinking.

**Cynthia** There was a common value too, in secularism?

**Pragna** Secular, yes, and I think socialist and feminist as well. But the focus on the racism and racist structures of the state was vital, because without that, how could we have held such an alliance together? We could have ended up saying that the rise of fundamentalist movements, which we were seeing most clearly and visibly and vociferously expressed in minority communities, was the problem. As opposed to the racism of the British state, with its privileging of Christianity, being exposed as the problem.

**Cynthia** Then WAF would have fallen onto the racist side of the knife edge it was always walking on. So that thing that Nira said (see p94) about transversal politics involving three things - position, identity and values - what you're saying

---

1. In January 1999 Women Against Fundamentalism was renamed Women Against Fundamentalisms, in the plural, and is operating as an e-mail list and currently developing a Web site. For further information contact the following e-mail address: waf-l@gn.apc.org

---

is that the values are really important. That it was vital, finding that combination of opposition to political religious projects *and* anti-racist politics that held WAF together?

**Pragna** Absolutely.

**Cynthia** Just now in Britain there's a new attempt to mobilise a civil rights movement. Do you see SBS and WAF feeding into this?

**Pragna** The attempt to build a civil rights movement just now is coming out of this momentous case, the Stephen Lawrence case. It's given rise in the last two years to an extraordinary public debate on racism and the state. The debate's been generated by the sheer determination and courage of Stephen's parents, Neville and Doreen Lawrence, and a number of committed lawyers and anti-racist activists, all of whom have worked tirelessly to force his killers to answer for their actions. In particular we've seen an unprecedented public interrogation of the nature of police investigation of racial crimes, bringing to the fore yet again the concept of institutionalised racism and lack of police accountability. The case is all the more extraordinary for striking a chord across all sections of society, including the right-wing media. But most notably amongst all sections of the various black communities. It's as if a space has opened up and a need to seize the opportunity is clearly recognised by a lot of people in the anti-racist movement, who are tentatively attempting to develop it into a civil rights movement. The question then is, well, how do we seize that moment? The trouble is as a civil rights movement it's being defined around that one particular issue.

**Cynthia** And the connection between racist violence and sexual violence? Is that recognised? Have they invited you or other women's projects to share in the organising?

**Pragna** It's a good question. No, they haven't involved us. The debates on the content and direction of the movement seem to be taking place behind closed doors and involving black, largely male anti-racist activists and some lawyers. The initiative doesn't appear to involve in any meaningful way progressive black or white feminists or other groups and movements like the trade union movement, gays and lesbians and refugee organisations. And when I brought this up with them (and it's classic, Marie, you'll laugh when I tell you this), when I told them 'You've got to be inclusive, that's what my notion of a civil rights movement is all about, its inclusiveness', their response was, 'Well, six months down the line when we've got this bit on race right, we'll broaden out.'

**Marie** So you just hold on there for your freedom because that'll come somewhere down the line.

**Cynthia** Women have to wait again. So the new civil rights movement is addressing one very terrible kind of violence that happens to people in Britain, but it's ignoring another kind of endemic violence happening in Britain: domestic violence, rape.

**Marie** In 'Making Women Seen and Heard' I think what women were saying was, if PAFT was a tool to challenge the decision-making, then as well as using it on behalf of their own particular interest group they would want to use it to challenge the kind of process that makes domestic violence such a non-event on the agendas of political parties. I think domestic violence is the issue that challenges all the tiers of patriarchal domination in society at once. The family, the community, the judiciary, the state, every tier gets hit there. And it's such an intimate thing for women too. On the International Day against Violence against Women last December I addressed a rally outside the Dail, the Irish Parliament, called by Irish Women's Aid. They'd very cannily thought up the theme 'We're calling for a ceasefire on domestic violence'. They asked me to put domestic violence in the framework of the ceasefires and the peace process. And what I suggested is: why shouldn't women in Ireland, North and South, be demanding that one of the new cross-border bodies provided for in the Peace Agreement be on domestic violence?

**Pragna** Yes, the Irish experience tells us so clearly, and we've seen it in Bosnia too, that violence is a spectrum. There are links between military rape and domestic violence. And there are links between racist violence and domestic violence. And yet here we are, stuck with a civil rights movement that's just getting off the ground that can't see that, because it refuses to allow dialogue with groups that would enable the connections to be made.

**Cynthia** So to be effective a civil rights movement has to be a broad coalition confronting different forms of oppression?

**Pragna** Absolutely. And it's not enough either for a movement to consider itself democratic simply by virtue of having in it 'representatives' from the gay and lesbian community, the trade union movement, disability organisations and so on, in a check-list kind of tokenism. It's about content. The coalition needs to reflect different forms of oppression by finding ways of overcoming the difference of *agenda* that different forms of oppression give rise to, identifying some kind of common set of demands or values that we can all subscribe to.

I think it's a tall order, perhaps it's totally unrealistic and perhaps none of us are reading the moment very well. But it seems to me that's the way in which we ought to be moving. There's not that many great examples about, but I think that one of the most inspiring things for me was seeing Jesse Jackson's rainbow coalition-building attempts in the US back in the 1980s. How well it would have succeeded I don't know, but it was a good example of the potential existing for a democratic collective, made up of disparate groups. That's the only hope there is, to rise above the kind of single issue and ghettoised politics that all of us are submerged in in our day to day work.

So there are serious problems. I don't think that a practice of transversal politics is common currently within the anti-racist movement. It's very new I think even amongst women. But to me what transversal politics is *not* about is 'Let's deal with this oppression first, then we'll deal with everything else'. Precisely because transversal politics has learned from those dangers of identity politics. As women we always situate our demands within a wider framework and analysis of what goes on, so it's not limited to an understanding of men and women only. Even though we focus around women's issues, there are insights that we're bringing in from different movements, and we're always situating our demands within something much wider, whether it's using human rights language which women are beginning to do, or linking with other movements.

**Marie** I think we need to be very systematic in a social movement. We have to ask ourselves precisely what change is encompassed within our demands. What are the targets, the outcomes we want? By what criteria shall we measure whether the change is taking place? What are the criteria for assessing how much different people are participating - because for the demands to be inclusive you need to be including many voices in making them.

**Cynthia** Marie, thinking back to 'Making Women Seen and Heard' and the more general movement you were describing for the implementation of PAFT principles in Northern Ireland - is that also incipiently a civil rights movement?

**Marie** It's not as structured as a civil rights movement, I wouldn't put it like that. But it's been very successful in terms of lobbying. And the moral high ground is ours really on this one, if we're looking at a new Northern Ireland, or a new Ireland, that's based on equality. Because we're saying, 'This is the means of doing it.' And 'fair treatment' is already on the statute books what's more.

And I certainly can't say I found it as difficult as Pragna's been describing. What I think made it work was that everybody knew that each of us was doing our damndest within our own constituencies to bring the issue forward, to bring it on, and each of us trusted the other to do that. There was Patrick Yu for ethnic minorities, Monica Wilson from the disability movement, a colleague from the Travellers, and we have ex-prisoners, one from the Loyalist side, one from the Republican side, who are now involved in grass roots community work. And UNISON and the trade union movement. And the pivot on which the whole movement hinges is the Committee for the Administration of Justice - the CAJ. It's a human rights non-governmental organisation, lawyers and others working at the grassroots level, servicing the community. They resource the various groups in the alliance, inform us about the legal implications of PAFT. They're able to translate from the legalese and bureaucratic language for us. And they inform us what human rights instruments are available to us that we may not have seen.

What would worry me about the new civil rights movement you're talking about in Britain is that because it has a singular demand, about racism, the state may be able to accommodate it without having to shift too much. It's not challenging the very basis of power relations. We saw this in the civil rights movement in Northern Ireland in the late 1960s, which was also organised around a singular demand: 'One man, one vote'. The state could have accommodated that. Mind you, at the time we had the kind of state that wasn't prepared to accommodate anything. But actually it could have. And if it had, we'd have probably chugged along for another thirty years without any serious changes. And if your demand of the state is about the complete reassessment of power relations, then those framing the demand have to be reassessing their own power relations.

**Pragna** Yes, it brings us back to that really key insight that it's only if the process is democratic that the outcome will be democratic. But if it is a broad coalition, if a civil rights movement is made up of many kinds of people who feel disenfranchised in various ways, gender or race or disability or sexuality or whatever, the challenge is creating a framework of demands that meets all those different needs. That should involve a huge exercise of consultation in every locality, the way you've attempted through PAFT. And if those demands, which would be about transformation of power, were met, everybody would benefit, not just one section of society at the expense of others. I can't even begin to imagine what such a collective set of demands would look like, but they would inevitably include devolving power from state to local level, they would be about transparency in decision making processes, about equality proofing in the way that you've talked about, and looming large in all of that, accountability within state institutions.

**Cynthia** It's interesting, because what you're both saying is that to make the kind of peace that you want, in Northern Ireland, and to make the kind of urban peace that you want, Pragna, you have to actually address a very wide agenda and bring a very wide coalition to bear on it. But look, there are two ways for projects like SBS and the Network to carry their struggle out onto a broader stage. One is to play a part in building social movements, the way you've just been describing. The other is to get women involved directly in politics-with-a-big-P, political parties and representative democracy. In the general discussion we had at the end of the 'Doing Transversal Politics' seminar quite a lot of women were saying, 'What about getting women into Politics?' How did you react to that?

**Marie** I think you'd want to apply the same criteria to engaging with the parties and the state as you'd apply to engaging with social movements. Is the process transparent? What constituency are you representing? How are you being accountable to them? If those questions were applied to mainstream politics I'd have no problem at all with women engaging in the political party system. Because that would change the way mainstream politics is done. It would be a bridge from participative to representative democracy. But instead, what happens when women go into mainstream politics is that once in the system they are lost to women on the ground. They themselves feel very isolated and unsupported. The communication breakdown is total and the resentments on both sides just build up. And so when women talk about 'going into mainstream politics' I'd much prefer they'd talk about what would be the process of changing *how* women go in, and how they act within it.

**Pragna** That's true whether it's women or black people, anybody. For those of us who work in black communities a deep rift opens up the minute people go into politics in the big-P sense, between those in the community and the politicians. Often those politicians have ridden into politics off the backs of various struggles that have taken place. They've got into power, they're supposed to be representative, but then there's a complete lack of accountability. You have to talk about some kind of structure of accountability.

**Cynthia** In Northern Ireland a Women's Coalition was formed to stand for election to the Northern Ireland Forum that laid the ground for a return to representative democracy. Can we learn anything from that experiment? Because that wasn't just women entering the old parties. They were making a new party, entering a new kind of representative process to build a new kind of parliamentary assembly. Have women been able to operate better in that innovatory situation?

**Marie** The trouble is the Women's Coalition was an initiative jump-started with the support of the Secretary of State at the time. The state no doubt saw it as a means of responding to criticisms of the 'democratic deficit' in Northern Ireland in terms of gender. But if the state had been really serious about getting women represented, a more democratic approach would have encompassed consultation with all the women's organisations on the basis: 'Could you all get together, we'll resource you to take some kind of women's initiative in this new forum. Could you consult and come up with some ideas about what you'd want.' That's not how it happened. It's not to say the women involved in the Women's Coalition haven't done some good work, in difficult circumstances. They are operating in a very male environment. But it was a top-down initiative, not a bottom-up initiative, and that's always the acid test.

**Cynthia** At the 'Transversal Politics' seminar I remember Nora Rathzel saying that projects like ours actually do play a part in mainstream politics, but not by putting women up for election. She said that mainstream politicians and parties can't achieve anything without getting their ideas through to ordinary people. And what projects like Southall Black Sisters and the Women's Support Network do is screen out, or act as a buffer against the ideologies and identities being pressed on us from above by making other kinds of values current among the people we work with.

**Pragna** I think that's right, and it's why we put so much effort into connecting with and mobilising women at community level, so we're not just talking to ourselves.

**Marie** And I think that the Network, being an umbrella structure with member organisations, gives us a reach that being a single central organisation we couldn't have. Because each member women's centre is a feeler, a tentacle if you like. And if there's 25 women's projects in the Network that's 25 tentacles, with lots of little sucker pads, advice services, education courses, child care or social events or whatever. Not every woman who comes in contact with a member group necessarily even remotely shares all the values. She may just use the service to meet a particular need and go away again. But for every five who do that, there's one that stays.

**Cynthia** It seems to me that the way both your projects do their work of blocking ideologies coming from above is by creating optional identities of resistance, putting into play identities that wouldn't otherwise be available to people. I think what you do is to make available what you might call a 'secular' identity, a way of avoiding the specific narrowing and fixing identities with which people are addressed by the state, by mainstream political forces, or by community or religious leaders. You provide a space where they can complain and be critical about their situation, redefine their sense of who they are, but without having to deny their belonging.

**Pragna** That's it. Because when women come to us they don't say 'Look, I've suffered domestic violence and from now on I'm just throwing my entire culture and religion out of the window because of what it's done to me.' What they do say is 'I've suffered violence. I need help and assistance. I reject certain parts of my cultural and religious identity, the part that imposes or condones violence. I don't actually recognise that as my culture. But I remain Hindu, or I remain Muslim, or I remain Sikh'. So they keep their celebrations and their lifestyles, making them what they wish them to be.

**Marie** I think the same thing happens in Northern Ireland. A lot of the desire for a secular space comes from those Protestants who are alienated from the orthodoxies of Protestant culture, the Orange Order and the Unionist Party. They desire something else to belong to, that they can feel comfortable with. And all of us benefit from that. It's a major contribution.

**Cynthia** And Catholics?

**Marie** I think Catholics step in and out of a secular space all the time. Some Catholics. Even for myself, other than the organised religious bit and the priests and the nuns, there's not a whole lot in the culture in being a Catholic that I'd want to reject. Because it's a culture of challenge, of questioning the state. I don't want to throw that baby out with the bathwater. But I do want to be part of something that doesn't define me solely as that. You talked about 'juggling identities' Pragna. (See 'Difficult Alliances', p117). That's what I want to be able to do, to juggle the identities of being a Catholic, being working-class, a woman, a lesbian - and not allowing any of those identities to have supremacy over the others.

**Pragna** And only a genuinely secular state can guarantee space for that.

# The values of community writing

## Rebecca O'Rourke and Lynette Hunter

*Rebecca O'Rourke* and *Lynette Hunter* describe the development of community writing in the UK and look at its relationship to transversal politics

Unlike the 'Doing Transversal Politics' Seminar at Gresham in January 1999, which grew out of several years of work with a core group of women, 'Translating Practices, Translating Words' brought together a range of cultural practitioners who in the main worked in isolation from each other. In bringing this range of writing projects together we wanted to do two things. First, to create the opportunity for the exchange of ideas and experiences between writing projects and activities which, although they may seem (and in many ways are) very different in terms of their focus and audience, have in common their challenge to the way writing is valued by dominant critical approaches in educational institutions. In all these projects, writing and creative activity is valued as a participatory activity. This is in contrast to both functional and consumer based approaches to writing and cultural activity which might otherwise have been the sum total of these people's engagements with words. Second, we wanted to begin a critical debate about the value and purpose of these participatory and productive projects, both individually and as a whole, as a means of exploring the creative tensions between culture and politics. In this article we sketch the lines of that critical debate. We do so both to provide context for the accounts of situated cultural-political work from practitioners which follow and to pose questions about the relationship between culture and transversal politics.

The article outlines the development of community writing in the UK and then highlights the issues concerning culture and transversal politics which bear on it. We explore these through the framing device of value, asking in turn what are the social, personal, political and aesthetic values of community writing.

## A brief history of community writing

Community Writing has been in common usage since the early 1980s to describe forms of writing and publishing, and forms of reading that writing, which exist outside the dominant literary and educational institutions and the relations of reading and writing which they maintain and promote. People who work on literature in these institutions are beginning to recognise the need to learn how to value the writing and oratory that goes on outside the narrow range of this dominant community, and this has been reflected for example in a substantial movement into looking at diaries, journals and autobiographies.

Taking a broad cut through history, we see that whenever literary relations have been institutionalised in a dominant form there have emerged (or continued) traditions of opposition and subversion. Their non-literariness has often been foregrounded and such traditions come down to us as folk, working-class or socialist traditions, or are reformulated as lost canons of women's, lesbian and gay or black writing and writers. In this sense community writing has a long and complex history, but its historical roots are generally identified with the new social movements of the late 1970s (feminism, direct-action community politics, non-labour movement forms of socialism) and their new sites of political intervention, especially neighbourhood. These new political forms were both dependent on and interested in cultural and educational practices as a way of linking political agency with consciousness and ideology.

Community writing retains the polemical sense of the word which Raymond Williams identifies when he talks about community politics: 'distinct not only from *national politics* but from formal *local politics* and normally involves various kinds of direct action and direct local organization.[1]

It originated with disaffected schoolchildren, adult literacy learners and the socially and educationally disadvantaged urban poor who became involved in forms of community education.[2] It was organised by two distinct purposes. First, to represent to and for themselves, as well as to the mainstream, areas of experience and knowledge which were marginalised, silenced or profoundly misrepresented. Second, to argue with the mainstream - in the form of the Arts Council, compulsory education system and the media - about definitions of literature and literary value.[3] At the same time a related, but quite different, challenge to education, writing and publishing from feminists was taking place.[4]

These political engagements with culture throughout the 1970s and 1980s created a series of changes to literature policy and writing in education, both compulsory and post-compulsory, which opened up wider opportunities for participation in writing activities. They were characterised by their emphasis on participation, as opposed to appreciation, and on diversity and inclusivity,

---

1. Raymond Williams, 1982, p66.
2. Chris Searle and Ken Worpole were both school teachers in London's East End who responded to the lack of relevant and meaningful reading books for their students by encouraging them to write and print their own. Ken Worpole went on to found Centerprise Publishing Project, one of the founder-members of the Federation of Worker-Writers and Community Publishers (FWWCP). Jane Mace, Sue Gardener, Patricia Duffin and Stella Fitzpatrick were all active in the radical literacy movement of the 1970s and founder members of *Write First Time*, a national magazine produced by and for adult literacy students. Scotland Road and Liverpool 8 Writers, also founding members of the FWWCP, developed from Liverpool University's innovative community education projects. See K. Worpole and D. Morley (eds), *The Republic of Letters* (1982); and J. Thompson, *Adult Education for a Change* (1980).
3. Throughout the 1970s and 1980s the FWWCP was engaged in a series of arguments with the Arts Council about its funding policy for literature. This was partly an argument about accountability - how and for whom the money was spent - but it was also an argument about value and definition. On many occasions during this period there were attempts by the Literature Director to divert applications to the then newly established Community Arts Panel. These were always resisted by the FWWCP which was seeking to challenge the elite definitions of literature and literary value which held sway in the Arts Council at that time.
4. The two movements share many similar features and several women worked with and for both movements but there were significant differences. Here it is most relevant to note the extent to which feminism was able to develop a commercial base for feminist initiatives in writing and publishing. Commercial publication and distribution on this scale has never been an option for working-class and community writing and publishing.

and their interest in the process as well as the product of writing. The term community writing is an umbrella for the many different forms of engagement with writing and publishing these changes reflect, and several of the projects which took part in the seminar identify with the term. However, as noted earlier, apart from those writing projects which are members of networking organisations (such as the Federation of Worker Writers and Community Publishers (FWWCP), the Association for the Literary Arts in Personal Development (LAPIDUS), the National Association of Writers in Education (NAWE) or the Voluntary Arts Network (VAN) there are few opportunities for members to learn from and about each other's existence. The winter 1998-9 edition of the FWWCP's magazine *Federation* contains a proposal to change its name to The Federation of Community Writers and Publishers. Debates about the organisation's identity, in relation to feminism and socialism, have been contentious in the past. Though not of direct concern here, the inclusion of feminism alerts us to how the practices of community writing are and have been gendered.

## Gendering community writing

Although feminism has been extremely successful in promoting contemporary and historical traditions of women's writing within education and publishing, it has been less successful in establishing networks which sustain women's writing at the level of the workshop, the community or region. Existing networks for community writing and writing development have many active, and often feminist, women and several women-only groups, but these are rarely organised solely on the basis of gender. MAMA, who contributed to the seminar and to this edition of the journal, came together on the basis of both gender and race and several women's writing groups which have formed as part of arts and health initiatives draw their membership from mental health system users and survivors. Gender issues are further complicated as some women-only groups have opened sessions or activities to men only to find they do not attend them.

The various writing networks referred to above are all gendered and racialised but none of them give especial importance to gender or other forms of separatism. There may be an element of gender-blindness at work in some cases but it is important to recognise that for some organisations this is a conscious political strategy.[5] Throughout the early 1980s the FWWCP engaged in a series of bitter debates about whether women's groups met the terms of membership. These were complex arguments, as they needed to be, which confronted the generally accepted middle-class bias of the UK women's movement in the 1970s and the patriarchal attitudes and chauvinism of the male working class and its labour movement. The debates continued long after their apparent resolution, when Women and Words were admitted as full members in 1982, and were the first of several painful and far-reaching explorations in the light of the new identity politics of race, sexuality and disability. Male and female members of the FWWCP today seek to respect and positively embrace difference of all kinds, including gender. Planning the seminar we discovered we held different assumptions about who it was for. The decision to restrict the conference to women was amicable, between ourselves and in the different community writing organisations we were in contact with, but was not without its contradictions. These included one project's disappointment at not being able to send its newly appointed male Family Literacy worker for the Asian and Afro-Caribbean communities and the importance to several contributors of stressing not only that they worked with men and women but that in certain situations the identities they shared with men mattered more to them than the differences. These highlight the difficulty with which gender issues can be seen as distinct and separate within community writing and they raise a question, too big to do more than flag here, about the scope for trans-gender transversal politics.

**Personal or social value?**

So far we have distinguished community writing and orality from hegemonic writing on the basis of its concern with participation, diversity and inclusivity. But these do not explain why, and to whom, it continues to be useful and valuable. In the sections which follow we argue that it widens the base of those participating in mainstream culture, contributes to a more equitable or representative common culture, and returns culture, and its role in the creation of meaning and identity, to a more broadly defined social location than it often

5.  Our knowledge of these organisations is not equal and this will be reflected in our comments. Rebecca is a member of FWWCP, NAWE and LAPIDUS but her different levels of involvement with each will affect her practical understanding of how they operate in relation to this issue.

inhabits. Our choice of the word 'useful' is deliberate, signalling a break with values of scarcity or exchange more traditionally associated with artistic activity. Community writing and orality is also distinctive for another reason, which bears on the broader relationships between culture and politics raised here: namely the way in which models of cultural production are so often individualistic in their focus and the challenge to this of co-operative and communal forms of artistic practice. But community writing does not just widen the pool of potential participators in mainstream cultural forms, and nor are its purposes limited to the literary or aesthetic. The way in which it encourages participation, builds individual and social confidence, and communicates across as well as within specific cultural situations, provides a model of how individuals become empowered and active within groups. This can then be extended to other areas of social and political activity.

In the accounts which follow we see that the content of particular writing, story telling or theatre activities makes a direct contribution to raising awareness about or validating the experience of specific social and cultural groups. But almost as important as the articulation and communication of this often hidden or marginalised knowledge is the accompanying process (which is always both an individual and a social act) of learning how to define and communicate these meanings in the broader social context of learning that power is intricately bound up with defining and communicating meanings. It is the interdependence of social, political and personal factors within this process which supports our claim that such uses of writing and orality are emancipatory. Sonia Linden, talking about the Write to Life writing residency at the Medical Foundation, explained that a life experienced as incoherent achieved coherence through the process of remembering, talking and writing (with or without a scribe) which the project made available. She stressed its cathartic value, noting that the writing was often concerned with details which had not been shared with others: 'Family are the last people they want to burden with these dark memories'.

The content of Nasrin's account of torture in Iran was profoundly personal, yet the context in which it took place was clearly social and political. The act of writing it down generated two very different kinds of value. For Nasrin, the experience released her from it in a very immediate way: it stopped the nightmares; it also achieved the aim she had first brought to the Write to Life project, that of raising awareness about the political regime under which she had suffered. For her, and for those of us listening to the account, there was no conflict between personal, social or political value, as their interrelatedness was clear. But in some contexts there can be conflict between social and personal use values.

We referred earlier to the way artistic practice can sit uncomfortably with politics because of the different relation each has to the individual and the group. This is heightened when therapeutic values and purposes are introduced. The stress on individual solutions to individual problems within therapeutic practices can lead to a situation where determination is obscured and social conflicts are experienced as personal problems.

**'We have systematic ways of attributing value to words: good and bad words, good and bad books, good and bad writers and readers'**

It is not inevitable that the use of writing and orality in arts for health, personal development and therapeutic contexts does this. In fact, work in the area of bibliotherapy in Canada and Australia often starts from precisely this challenge to such individualism and has worked in areas such as domestic violence, homelessness and chemical dependency which emphasise the social dimension of these experiences. Bibliotherapy takes seriously the idea that we 'write ourselves into existence'. It works with the basic premise that writing and reading help us to sort out events in our lives, understand and move past their destructive and diminishing patterns. In doing so it recognises - and works with the resulting knowledge - that the self we write into existence is a social self.

Celia Hunt and Urmilla Sinha, both active in LAPIDUS, provided an account of how writing empowers. Writing is of enormous value in generating the insights and confidence which sustain struggle for change in the material world. Their account of the writing process, recognised and affirmed by other writers present, is in many ways a paradigm of transversal politics. They described a series of writing techniques (switching from 1st to 2nd to 3rd person narration, transposing people and events and the accurate recall of geographical places and their emotional resonance) which allowed both writer and reader to move beyond the surface details of experience and enter its interior. The refinement of this technique allows writers to imaginatively

inhabit and create empathy with the experience of others. The writers' creed -
to show not tell - becomes in this context a powerful political and therapeutic
tool. The social uses of community writing and orality are, then, varied and
powerful, but within our culture it is impossible to talk about writing for very
long without coming up against questions of literary value.

## Decentering literary value

The seminar brought together women who shared uses of writing and orality
which both explored identity within the group and communicated with people
who identified differently. So what they are engaged in is 'translation' - sometimes
literally between languages, sometimes from oral to printed words, or from one
tradition of reading or community of readers to another. Translation always
involves producing something different without erasing the things that are
'difficult' about it. It also demands that we find words which will enable those
who read what is written to value it, both within their terms and ours, however
different these two things might be.

Most of us take words for granted. Human beings spend an immense
amount of time training young people in the use of words from a
very early age, not only in education but in our daily interactions as
we learn how to ask questions, respond to grief or talk out our anger, as well as
simply how to be kind. We go on learning about words in this way all our lives,
and so can forget that it's a highly skilled craft. It is often easier to see this
when something jars, perhaps when an English speaker, for example, listens to
someone from another English-language society speaking in a way they don't
understand or feel to be 'correct'. Language is not a neutral medium, but
reproduces and reflects its own relations of difference and power in ways which
make it a social and political weapon as well as a social and political tool. In
Britain we have systematic ways of attributing value to words: good and bad
words, good and bad books, good and bad writers and readers. The standards
against which words are measured have largely been devised and maintained
by people in privileged positions and their standards represent their concerns
and issues. These are as much a community of writing and writers as any other.
In questioning the dominance of their value system, and the writing it relates
to, we are not denying that the work, its writers or its readers exhibit the value
ascribed to it. What we question is the effect on all writing and writers of a

process which operates as if its values were absolute and universal.

Words written down become 'literature' if they have value. Listen to that phrase: if they have value. As if value were a fixed thing to be discovered like a seam of gold in a mine. You can only think of value in that way if you are sure your own standards for life are, or should be, the same as everyone else's. But is there a fixed and absolute definition of what is good and therefore valuable? We do not think so. We think that value is something we make. It is negotiated over and woven into our lives as we ask: valuable to whom, for what reasons, under what circumstances? Deciding on this kind of value is more difficult.

Why do we need to do so? Words, above all else, bring us together yet at the same time mark out our difference - without them we cannot have a democracy. This is why the areas of emancipatory writing and orality with which we are concerned here - life-writing, bibliotherapy, literacy, English as a second (or third, or fourth) language, oral history, community writing and theatre projects - are so important. Yet traditional literary value requires distance between our personal lives and our art, as if it were bad manners to talk about ourselves. In aesthetics, value is frequently associated with 'beauty' and 'rarity', as if something really well-made could only be made by a few people. As more and more people have the chance to work on words they do what all artists do, they write from experience. Excluding these voices from literary value means society denies itself the wealth of experience, the precious environments of existence and economies of survival, that these voices have so painstakingly worked out.

The voices provide a context for each other; the web of differences they share helps us untangle the complexity of the lives that are being told. MAMA's book *Shells on a Woven Cord*, like so many other community writing publications and projects, sweeps away the invisibility and silence that has surrounded their culture by the sheer volume of the collection, story after story putting into place a lost piece of life that needs valuing. Writer after writer gives testimony to the fact that they are writing not only or even primarily for themselves, but for their communities. And so it is with each community writing project where each individual adds their density and weight to the collective whole so that these diaries, letters, stories, poems and autobiographies demonstrate the variability of self, the questioning and ambiguity of identity, in which the speaking voice not only asks the reader, but also itself, what is trustworthy and what is of value.

# Theatre and reconciliation

## Gerri Moriarty and Jane Plastow

*Gerri Moriarty writes about community theatre in Northern Ireland, and Jane Plastow writes about the Eritrea Community-Based Theatre Project.*

## Working in Northern Ireland
### Gerri Moriarty

These are personal reflections from the writer, based mainly on work with Dock Ward Community Theatre Group (North Belfast) and Ballybeen Community Theatre Group (East Belfast).

*It is 1991. I am standing in the rain, in the dark, under a road bridge in the New Lodge, North Belfast. I am waiting with about 40 other people, aged between 10 and 65, mostly Catholic, some Protestant. We are waiting for the police and army to defuse a suspect car bomb. We are waiting to go to rehearsals for a community play …*

*It is two weeks later. St. Kevin's Church Hall is packed to capacity, with an audience waiting to watch the history of their area unfold on stage. As the lights go down, shooting starts in the streets outside. The cast and the audience carry on their journey together …*

*It is 1992. The Dock Ward Community Theatre group are devising a play on contemporary themes, exploring what the conflict has meant to them. A young man comes up to talk to me after a workshop. He says, 'All of us have different ideas about what's going on here and about how it might be changed. But in the workshop, there's a safe place for us all to talk about it and to listen to each other' …*

It is 1995. I am on the North Antrim coast with a group from the Protestant Ballybeen estate, devising material for their community play, 'The Mourning Ring'. One of the women in the group begins, 'We walked up the hill this morning to Layde churchyard and looked at the graves'. We begin to speak together of death and loss, of mourning and betrayal …

It is 1996. I am talking to one of the women from Ballybeen Community Theatre. She has been taking part in a community play in a Catholic area. 'I was afraid going in in case they'd shoot me because I was a Prod, and I was even more afraid going home in case they'd shoot me because they knew where I'd been' she tells me …

It is 1999. I am working with Catholics and Protestants from across Belfast on the devising of 'The Wedding', a community play which looks at the issues surrounding the marriage between a Catholic and Protestant. A group of young girls chant abuse at the bride's brother, a woman freezes as she finds out that her new son-in-law's family are 'involved', an older woman speaks of her loneliness at cutting off contact with her community after her own 'mixed' marriage, a mother-in-law bitches about the inferior quality of the wedding presents given by the 'other' side. An older man comes up to me at the end of the workshop. He says 'I keep telling our ones. This is a safe space, where you can be what you want to be' …

Over nearly a decade, the gift which community theatre can offer - the gift of a safe space where individuals and groups can explore difference, can question, can say the unsayable, can look at the terrifying and the terrible (as well as the funny and the everyday, the tender and the passionate) - seems to me to grow in significance rather than diminish.

On the one hand, there is nothing very mysterious about this gift. Community theatre has developed many techniques which support participants and audiences in the process of self revelation, analysis and discovery. Drama games and exercises help people across the limiting boundaries of politeness, inhibition, wariness, encouraging risk-taking, collaboration, humour. Drama improvisations examine conflicts, push for new challenges, allow a range of voices to be given expression. Image-making and story-telling allow us to find other layers of truth - the truth of our emotions, the truth of the observed detail, the truth trapped in our physical bodies as well as in our over-worked brains and tongues. And endless hours of conversation over pints or cups of tea help us to consolidate and extrapolate from what we have learned.

And, in performance, we have been able to use the infinitely variable language of theatre to ask our audiences to consider new possibilities, find different perspectives, whilst at the same time holding on to some security in the familiar. So, in St. Kevin's church hall in North Belfast, the audience were seated in the round, under sycamore branches in the shape of a crown of thorns. In Dundonald High School, in East Belfast, the audience sat on opposite sides of a traverse stage. They watched each other's reactions as much as the stage action, which shifted between the sixteenth and twentieth century. And for 'The Wedding', the audience will be taken by bus from a house in a Catholic area, to a house in a Protestant area, to a chapel or church, to a wedding reception, in our own version of promenade theatre.

Community theatre has also offered opportunities to share with others living outside our immediate communities. Groups have toured to Enniskillen and Letterkenny, to Dublin and the West of Ireland. Women from the North have exchanged views and experiences at seminars and conferences with women from the South and from other countries. With each journey away from home, our understanding of ourselves is extended, our knowledge of the 'other' expanded.

There have been many difficulties. With every bomb, or punishment beating, with every tortuous twist and turn of the political process, the safety of participation in community theatre has to be re-evaluated. We have had to consider cancelling rehearsals and performances, we have had to consider stopping projects half-way through, we have had to delay plans for projects until the climate was more favourable. The questions we ask are endless. If we rehearse in this venue or that venue, will it be regarded as 'neutral' territory? If this writer is asked to help with the script, will his/her gender, perceived religious affiliation or politics prove a barrier to honest communication within the group? How will this scene, or this stage design be read by audiences who are both politically sophisticated and highly literate in the language of symbol and metaphor? Have we been as truthful as we can be? Have we avoided difficult themes or ideas? Have we taken enough care of each other as the process unfolded? Have we failed technically to communicate as well as we might have done? What is the wider impact of our work? Sometimes we succeed, sometimes we fail bravely, and sometimes we fail dismally.

It is not a mysterious process and yet it is also a mysterious process. At its best, I have seen community theatre reach into the collective unconscious and make an imperceptible emerging reality visible. At its best, it offers its participants and audiences a meeting-point, a space at the cross-roads, a chance to ask difficult questions.

Two years ago, when I was working in East Belfast on a piece of research, a Protestant community activist gave me a phrase which became the title for my report: 'Walking new roads, stepping in new shoes'. The road from the bridge in the New Lodge has been new and demanding; for myself and for many of the individuals who have chosen to walk it, it is community theatre that has given us the spring in our step.

## Unity in diversity: the Eritrea Community-based Theatre Project
Jane Plastow

I don't know when the Eritrean liberation struggle first adopted the slogan 'Unity in Diversity', but it was certainly current in the 1980s as part of the EPLF (Eritrean People's Liberation Front) strategy for overcoming the history of divide-and-rule policies encouraged by successive colonial oppressors: Italians, British and finally Ethiopian. It has also been part of the fabric of the project I devised with the Eritrean Bureau of Cultural Affairs from our first discussions in 1992; it was an axiom I never thought about in great theoretical detail before encountering the idea of transversal politics, because it seemed such an obvious and sensible response to the issue of bringing together, valuing and promoting understanding in Eritrea's nine ethnic groups.

The armed Eritrean liberation struggle began in 1961 when Ethiopia tried to make Eritrea a province. Moreover in the early years of the struggle the Eritreans themselves were not united; and in the late 1970s two liberation fronts, the Muslim dominated ELF (Eritrean Liberation Front) and the more Christian, Tigrinya, Marxist-influenced EPLF, conducted a vicious civil war at the same time as the liberation struggle.

After winning the internal battle - which still leaves many ELF ex-fighters feeling embittered and disenfranchised - the EPLF had to find a way to pull Eritreans together as a nation. I suspect this was easier to do because there was such an obvious, genocidal 'other' around which to focus the unity campaign. Indeed, the war with Ethiopia has recently re-opened, and it has not escaped a number of commentators that this may be in part - on both sides - a response to the threat of a fracturing in national unity once the external 'other' had ceased to be such an urgent force for national unity. For military leaders the transition to the competing demands of burgeoning democracy is always difficult to negotiate, and war against an outsider offers a much simpler binary around which to unite the people and rule.

Ethnic strife has been and continues to be a source of trauma in many colonially created African nations. The leaders of the EPLF needed to find a way to avoid such a source of schism, and to promote understanding of different cultures amongst people as diverse as the animist Kunama of western Eritrea and the strictly Muslim Rashaida of the eastern coast, who would never normally have encountered each other, and had little obvious reason to embrace in any kind of national unity. Political speechifying is generally dull. Most Eritreans were illiterate and few had access to any kind of mass media. So the cultural weapon was invoked, in this case through the medium of the performative arts. Cultural troupes were established, both full and part time, amongst the fighters, amongst children, and even amongst groups such as disabled fighters, prisoners-of-war and women-only troupes. Some thirty per cent of the Eritrean fighting force was made up of women. Most of Eritrea's traditional societies were significantly oppressive of women, and so their part in performances was most important in a liberation movement committed to improving women's rights and standing in society.

The troupes produced variety shows consisting of propaganda and educational music, dance, and later, increasingly, neo-naturalistic drama productions, both to encourage the war effort and to promote understanding of the EPLF's wide-ranging programme of social reform. The third strand to this programme was the promotion of appreciation of the cultural forms and diversity of Eritrea's ethnic groups. In all the major troupes, which usually consisted of about thirty performers, attempts were made to recruit people from as many ethnic groups as possible, and the dances and music of all those groups were a key part of each troupe's repertoire. This element of the shows was always popular, but its political imperative was the promotion of mutual valuing of the cultures of different people.

It was against this background of a strong awareness of the importance of the cultural tool in creating both a nation and a more equitable society, and of a commitment to maintaining and valuing cultural diversity, that I was invited to contribute to the development of theatre in the post-liberation period. I met Alemseged Tesfai, Eritrea's premier playwright, veteran fighter, and leader of the cultural division of the Ministry of Education, in 1992. He wished his people to have the chance to see and learn from a whole range of kinds of performance, but he particularly wanted a way to develop Eritrean theatre as a form which would be representative of the national commitment to unity in diversity. He had never heard of the kind of syncretic community theatre, bringing together indigenous cultural forms with international progressive ideas about inclusive performance, which had been developed in other parts of Africa since the 1970s, and we discussed how such an idea might work as a more truly national theatre than any theatre based in a single building could.

Three years later, the Eritrea Community-Based Theatre Project was born. It has since conducted major training projects with three ethnic groups and with a pilot teacher training group, has sponsored four Eritreans coming to England for further training, and has organised three major tours of indigenous works, reaching maybe a quarter of the population, as well as resulting in the first community promenade performance in the village of Sala'a Daro. The form of theatre promoted under the initiative is also reaching far into the artistic infrastructure of Eritrea as trainees from the projects return to their own amateur and professional groups, and in 1997 a development play directed and devised by one of our first trainees won the country's premier artistic award.

A snapshot description may help give a picture of the work. In July 1996 I went to see a production of two plays which were then on tour in a remote town on the southern border with Ethiopia. The twelve actors were all graduates of our first, 1995, training programme. They had been on tour for two months, travelling on local buses and occasionally by camel to reach the most remote villages. They were putting on a play originally devised as part of the training, about land rights and reconciliation, and another they had devised entirely

*Above:: 'Mother arguing with son'. Land, Eritrea 1995.*
*Below: Community play in Sala'a Daro, the 'Angel Tree' scene. Eritrea 1997.*

autonomously, about the abuse of the custom that women must be virgins at marriage and about the iniquities of the bride-price system.

The performance site was an open area at the bottom of a steep hillside, and the plays, each about an hour long, were to be performed in the early evening when everyone had finished work. During the afternoon I sat with the actors in various bars, before we moved out to set up the two floodlights, connected to an ancient generator, and to establish a loosely circular arena as the performance space. As always, the children came first, but gradually they were joined by more and more adults, numbers of whom had walked up to two hours to see the plays. The audience chatted amongst themselves, sitting on the boulders of the hillside until eventually some two thousand people had arrived. Then came a song, a Tigrinya song celebrating the end of the war, and the actors came through the audience, in role, to dance and celebrate the victory of Eritrea. Two narrators punctuated the play with a comic, yet deeply important debate about who had land rights in the new Eritrea, where thirty years of war had given people deeply different experiences; with those who stayed at home, those driven into exile and ex-fighters, all seeking an inheritance in the new state. There was lots of slapstick, lots of physical acting and lots of music as the play debated the new land rights promulgated by the government. When you have to communicate with people half-way up a hillside you can't be too subtle in acting style and a good strong voice is extremely important. As the performance played on I moved about on the dark hill, avoiding the crush around the actual playing area, and watching the people watching the play. Bursts of laughter punctuated continual murmured voices as the audience discussed amongst themselves what was going on; and half way through I was brought back to sense of continuity and history when I looked down to the dirt road and saw the age-old sight of a camel train walking silently into town under the stars.

No one in the audience had seen a play like this before, which combined indigenous music and dance performance forms with ideas we had gleaned from a raft of international sources; including direct address to the audience, use of narration and characters who could step in and out of part in order to bring the audience into the action of the play.

The next day before we left, small boys kept coming around, singing snatches of the songs from the performance. The actors were happy. It had been a good show, though a fairly average audience by their standards - the biggest they reckoned had been around seven and a half thousand people. But the tour continued, and I saw them off on the bus which would take them to the next Tigrinya village and the next show the following evening.

The idea behind the training is not primarily to teach people to be actors. What we seek to provide is a democratic, inclusive way of thinking about the work. At the same time we aim not at a style of production, but what I refer to as a tool-kit of possible performance modes out of which trainees can eventually pick what they think to be most appropriate to their needs.

Initially we play a lot of games. These are fun; they relax people and enable them to begin to inter-relate, whilst building physical awareness, concentration skills and imagination. We also work with yoga, exercise and voice skills. Most of the people we have worked with in Eritrea begin by being very physically tense; and relaxation techniques are both therapeutic and essential to performance skills. As we move on to creating images of people's lives and aspirations the work can often become traumatic. Stories begin to emerge of the atrocities nearly everyone experienced during the war years, as well as deeply moving tales of female genital mutilation and rigid feudal structures which have in various ways curtailed individual freedoms. These stories are hard for us all to negotiate, but they are what usually becomes the bedrock of the plays we later devise; and the valuing of individual stories is an important element in building confidence and creativity.

Interestingly, some of our problems have centred around our insistence on using traditional forms of performance. It was only when the work actually came into performance and performers were able to see how people related to indigenous material as opposed to alien 'naturalistic' acting, that such an approach was really embraced. Many people, whilst proud of their cultures, know very little of them in any depth. The colonialists and the war between them have robbed the young of their cultural inheritance. In 1997 we were working on Tigre and Bilen cultures, and we were amazed to find huge differences in the variety of songs and dances that people knew, and an almost total lack of knowledge of the original significance of various dance forms. Both students and researchers had fascinating times performing regional varieties of dance and song to each other and debating their significance, as well as discussing just how important various elements of traditional culture - which can often be reactionary, especially towards women - was in creating modern performance and indeed the modern nation. In every case it would appear that it is this traditional material which, particularly in the predominantly rural areas, makes the material accessible to audiences and enhances their sense of ownership.

Training in performance and devising skills is fine, and the evidence to date seems to show that this kind of theatre is popular and feeds local debate on contemporary issues, but it is not enough. The second round of training, which began in 1997, is concerned with training the trainees to become community arts facilitators. The aim is to live and work in local communities, to enable them, and particularly the normally marginalised youth and women, to use performance as a means of voicing their own concerns. Ultimately we hope to set up a national network consisting of professional and amateur groups among all the ethnic groups to voice their needs, value their cultures and communicate to each other through relevant, dynamic, issue-based theatre.

I had worked in a number of African countries before going to Eritrea, but the joy of working with rather than against a government, and the huge enthusiasm of people to learn, as well as the palpable impact the theatre has made, has meant that the Eritrean Community Based Theatre Project has been a uniquely exciting learning experience.

# Sharing stories

## MAMA East African Women's Group

*Somalian women's stories*

### The development of MAMA

MAMA began in 1990 when five women who had left Somalia and moved to Sheffield met regularly at each other's homes exploring, sharing and discussing a whole range of issues which were specific to East African women living in the UK and in East Africa. From this gathering, these women embarked on a new journey, searching for opportunities for themselves and other women in similar circumstances.

Inspired by the wealth of experience drawn from the gathering, the group launched what is now the MAMA East African Women's Group. We grew steadily in numbers and by 1993 it was clear that we needed a space to discuss, share, plan and act collectively. From 1993 we started meeting at the Gap Women's Centre rather than our homes. Sharing stories had always been a key feature of the gathering and of Somali culture. From discussing the experiences and issues facing the Somali community as a whole, and women in particular, we began increasingly both to look outwards and celebrate Somali culture.

Our first venture was to start writing down some of the stories women told at our gatherings. This gave us the idea of putting these stories together in a book and the confidence and unity of our group encouraged us to approach publishers and funders in order to share our work more widely. *Shells On A Woven Cord*, our first publication, was launched in 1995. In 1997 the group launched their second book *How The Meat Was Divided*, a collection of Somali folk tales fully illustrated by Somali and African Caribbean children and young people. MAMA is now in the process of publishing their third book, *Footprint*. The foot symbolises the future and the past in the continuing journey of life presented within the context of Somali culture. Our book depicts the lives and stories of women through the theme of the Sar. Sar is an ancient belief which celebrates the unseen spirit connecting all human experience. The stories at the end of this piece come from this book, which will be published in 1999.

## The beat

The beat of the drum, the songs and the dance that vibrate in the air celebrate the MAMA, the oldest kingdom of the Mingis, the mother of the Sar.

This is the ceremony where women share their womanhood, sisterhood and their kind. The space is their space and the spirit surrounds them.

There is peace in their minds, warmth in their hearts and coolness in their bodies. Their feet are rooted deep into the ground and their bodies rock. Their movements are strong and balanced and their touch is one of great gentleness.

They leave their shoes at the doorstep, along with hatred, envy, and grudges between them. Their tensions go once they enter the ceremony. They are relaxed with each other, knowing that they all have reasons for coming to the ceremony. Their feet rest on the colourful mats and rugs scattered on the sand floor.

## Somali women and words
## Points from the 'Translating Practices' workshop

*Point 1 - We live on our words, we feed on our words.* Stories graze the mind. In the heat of the sun, on a long journey to the well, the mouth is a best friend/ companion and the words that come out of it are what keep the tired body and exhausted feet moving on. There is a song for building the house, story for travelling to the well, song for leaving a rude husband.

Through story telling and poetry women share information, embrace and empower each other and send messages and signals to each other. A woman who intends to leave her violent husband for example, sings herself a song or shares a story with her friends. Her song will say 'I see a path in the grains' and her story will say 'my shoes are strong'. Her friends will know what she means. (See *Recipe for leaving a rude husband*, below.)

*Note*: the story telling and poetry often works with the small things in day to day life, it captures the little things and turns them into signals.

*Point 2 - Gathering and celebrating.* Women also use their stories as a way to gather and celebrate and by doing this they ask and respond, give advice, and share ideas, knowledge and skills. They have their ways of expressing and explaining, describing, in which they may use characters of animals, plants, the importance of a vessel they use to keep their water, which they compare with the character of men. (See *Recipe for recognising bad men*, below.) In this story a young woman needs and seeks the advice and guidance of an older woman who tells her to be watchful of certain men.

*Point 3 - Women and language* There is a significant body of women's stories, poetry and songs, which play a key role in the shaping of day to day existence and the challenges of Somali women's lives. Yet women's literature is far less widespread and given less status than men's. In the past and even today language has been used to oppress women. Men's poetry in particular has been used to discourage, demoralise and sometimes shame women. When women challenged this they faced hostility and poetry of the most cruel manner.

*Note*: women's poetry and writing is not found in public, it is not taught in schools, or held in libraries. A young Bedouin woman came to challenge men with her poetry and she was attacked by poems to ensure that she did not succeed. The poems attacked even the private parts of her body so she was shamed.

*Point 4 - What translation means to us* The word for translation in the Somali language is turjun which is an Arabic word brought by Arab traders and missionaries. Prior to this word there was, and is still, an explanation rather than a word for translate in the Somali language, which is Af celi: exchange mouths. 'Exchange mouths' means negotiate and act as a mediator so that the matter being discussed is solved and understood rather than put into a word to word translation.

*Note*: When the English came into Somalia they imposed their language, but in the end they were not successful because they were not of the Islamic religion. Before this, the Arabs had also brought their language and imposed it, and far more successfully because they also brought Islam. But the Abyssinian Empire never did impose its language, it worked with a different kind of politics that kept Somali private, and when the Empire was lost everything was lost because no language was left behind.

## Storytelling

In Somalia we used storytelling as a way of expressing our understanding of the world around us. As part of our living in our new environment, the UK, we continue to use our stories to make sense of where we are, for example when writing our recipe for bargaining we express the contrast between the market in Hargeisa and Safeway in Sheffield. Somali women tell their stories not only in the celebration of the Sar but in different forms and shapes. A woman may build her story into her house, into a dance, or into embroidery or the weaving called *kabad*. These stories deal with a wide range of issues like friendship, feelings, changes, challenges, the environment, family and the community around. The four pictures we reproduce here, one kabad and three embroideries, each tell stories. We would like to explain the stories that these pictures tell.

## Kabad

Kabad is the material that acts as a decoration or as insulation in the aqal (house), which women weave. Each kabad is unique, reflecting the personality, character and spirituality of the woman who has woven it. The story each woman builds into her kabad can only be understood or explained by that woman and it's entirely up to her to share it or keep it a secret.

The knowledge and skills which women learn to create the kabad are recognised as a form of wealth. In decorating her house with the various

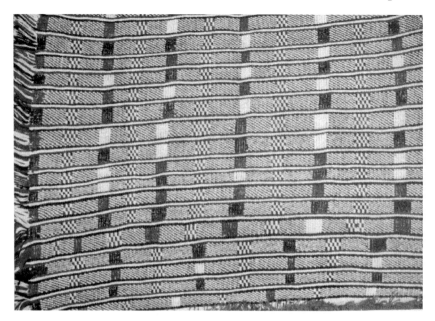

*Kabad*

embroidered and woven textiles, a woman demonstrates that she has strong links with older members of the community:

> She looked up at the ceiling, at the coloured plaits. It seemed to her the very fabric of her home was filled with all the answers to her questions, that all she had to do was sit quietly and listen, that in each twist and knot of string there was a story, perhaps the story of another woman in another time ...

The patterns on the kabad tell many stories. The large chequered squares represent the 'footprint of the fox'. In Somali culture, the fox is frequently associated with the woman, and it is said that the fox 'has a woman's mind'. In stories, women treat the mythical fox with suspicion, mistrustful of its intentions. Many stories tell of challenges between the fox and a woman and how the fox continually tries to catch the woman out to show she is careless or a poor home-maker. The presence of the fox's footprint in the kabad is a constant reminder to the woman that she be vigilant.

The solid lines on the kabad symbolise the udub which are the central pillars in the aqal. They represent strength, support, faith and belief and are also an inspiration to be strong and steadfast - something to hold on to and to depend upon. The close knit checks represent abundance, fertility, wealth, a desire for spiritual blessing and a wish for a good future. The colours of the kabad are also important. Red is frequently used to represent the spirit; it is a 'royal' colour, strongly linked to the spirit world. Green represents purity and nature.

## The Sar dance

The Sar is an ancient belief which can be traced back to the Ancient Egyptians and Abyssinians. Whilst other beliefs have been lost in time, the Sar remains important to Somali women. The Sar energy can heal the mind and body, and traditionally women will call upon the Sar to help them solve their problems and give them renewed strength. The Sar exists in a spiritual kingdom of tribes, communities and families.

Families choose their Sar as their link to the spiritual world. They celebrate their Sar with special ceremonies which will include dancing, sharing gifts, offering special food and drinking coffee which is the sacred drink of the Sar. At the beginning and during the ceremony they will burn incense to welcome the Sar. 'The Sar can give us much assistance and help.

*The Sar dance*

They help the women with their lives by solving their problems'.

This cloth would be used for decoration as a wall hanging, table cloth or pillow case. The design embroidered on to it tells the story of a dance to celebrate the Sar. Whilst the circles represent the women who dance and eat in circles during the celebrations, the circles also symbolise the individual women in the dance. The circles all touch, representing the spiritual links which bind the women together in the celebration. At the beginning of the dance, the women will have called the Sar, invoking the spirits to join them in the dance.

The flowers on the cloth represent the Sar who have responded to the women's invitations. The flowers are touching the circles and the women and the Sar are dancing together. They dance together for a long time, often until the Sar enters the women's bodies and they become one. The 'waves' which surround the circles represent the energy and joy which flows through the dance and the women's hearts. The spirit and the women connect to create a happy, exuberant and joyful atmosphere to celebrate the Sar.

*Trust and friendship*

## Trust and friendship

This cotton hand-embroidered cloth would be used in many ways in the aqal - as a wall hanging, pillow case, curtain, table cloth etc. The pattern illustrates the bond of friendship and trust Somali women share.

In Bedouin culture, life is about moving and travelling. A person may spend a season sharing the same piece of land, sharing food, water, secrets, conversations and possessions with another person. They may share the task of herding and milking their animals, and then move on in different directions for the following season in search of water and grazing. The woman who embroidered this cloth wished to represent the power of the unity and sharing she has experienced in friendships with other women whilst sharing a piece of land.

The three undulating patterns represent three women friends who have shared the same piece of land. They are all linked to illustrate the bond of trust they share in memories of past conversations, secrets, and the way they carried out their everyday lives together. The centre undulating pattern represents an older woman who brings wisdom and honour to their bond. She is the centre of the pattern, bringing everything together. The flowers which are interwoven within the women are celebratory and joyful to express the women's happiness.

The three strips surrounding the women represent 'pillars'. The pillar is a recurring symbol which suggests strength, stability, power, continuity and support. The rich colours represent the spiritual wealth of the women, their purity, their inner strength and their connection with nature.

## The Footprint

The embroidered pattern tells a story. The footprint symbolises a journey. An actual journey, journey of life, growing up, facing challenges, choices, moving through the stages of life.

*The Footprint*

The foot itself represents the whole body. For nomadic people the foot has great importance - 'you are as strong as your feet'. The foot represents strength, hope and ambitions. Leading from the foot is the spine which connects the foot to the head. The head guides the foot, finding the way forward and guiding the foot on the journey. In this context, the head also represents the future and is a link to the spiritual world.

The story of the footprint is a legend, passed down through generations: A woman flees her cruel husband and travels with her baby on her back through a desert to seek a refuge. It is a perilous journey, there are wild beasts around, there is no food and there are tales of a vicious lion who also poses a great threat to her and her child.

After some time, it begins to rain and she takes shelter in some bushes. Darkness falls and she suddenly hears branches snapping outside the shelter. She sees the ghostly figure of a lion and is so afraid she faints. When she comes round she sees the lion but he reassures her by patting the ground with his right paw to show her that he means her no harm. The woman understands the lion's gesture and now feels safe. She spends the rest of the night with the lion protected from any predators.

How can she be eaten by a hyena when a lion is protecting her.

The next morning she continues her journey, accompanied by the lion, until she comes to a small village. The villagers offer her refuge, refreshments and a place to stay. The lion has guided her to safety and now they have arrived, he leaves her. He pats the ground three times to say goodbye and leaves her.

The lion was not a predator, but represents an ancestor, watching over her and protecting her through her dangerous journey. In Somalia, when a lion is encountered it is not wise to confront it before being sure it is not the spirit of one of your ancestors.

## Stories from '*Footprints*'

### Recipe for leaving a rude husband

> *Tools:*
> *Maahmaah*, proverb
> *Hees*, a song
> *Bun*, coffee
> *Kabo adag*, strong pair of shoes
> *Qayd*, robe
> *Timir* (*sahay*), some dates

> *Ingredients:*
> *Ruuxaaga*, yourself
> *Nin*, husband

Remember the proverb 'silic ku nool sagaal nin guursataa dhaanta', better marry nine than put up with the insults and abuses of one;

> Never doubt yourself;
> Drink more coffee in honour of your Sar;

Sing yourself a song 'I see a foot print in the grains'
Tell him 'my shoes are strong'
'my shoes are ready'
'the path in front stretches'
'my shoes are at the door step'
'I am standing with my toes'
Tie a robe around your waist;
Take enough to tie to the tassels;
Take your first stride;
Don't look back;
Quicken your base;
You never know what's ahead of you.

## The woman Sado

Sado has come to Ardo looking for a safe place to keep, store her secrets. Two seasons ago she was separated from a friend with whom she had shared every secret. The women's family moved away (*geediyo*) in search of water and grazing. Sado has come to the ceremony to find *qof ay xog iyo xaal wadaagaan*, someone who would replace her friend, who would treasure her *sir*. Someone who, as she talks, would hear, nod, listen, agree, sympathise.

Sometimes only using *gacmahooda* and *wajigooda*, the women whisper to one another, saying words like:

'*Afkeenu waa isu amaan*'
'Our mouths are in peace'
'*Cadaygaagu yuu ogaan*'
'Don't even let this slip to the twig you clean your teeth with.'
'*Afku yuu kaa xadin*'
'This musn't be thefted of your mouth'
'*Dibneheenu way xidhan yihiin*'
'Our lips are sealed'

Like many other women at the party, Sado treats age as a precious secret and treasures it. Only her family and trusting friends know how old she is. She has come to tell Ardo that next season she will be *soddon jir*, thirty years old. Sado has another secret. She met a man at the well and needs Ardo's *talo*, her advice.

While Sado talks, Ardo sits in front of her, listening, nodding and rocking her head. She repeats the words and phrases 'only me, you and Eebe hear this', to make Sado feel comfortable with her inner feelings and reassure her that her secrets are safe.

Listening to Sado, Ardo has her own secret to tell. She closes her eyes, takes a deep breath, makes her hands dance and counts her fingers. She repeats and stretches her words then slaps her hands together. She does this to express herself and demonstrate her honest feeling, emotions and the seriousness of what she is saying. Sometimes words aren't enough. Ardo gives her secret to Sado and begs her to keep it in her heart. This is the secret Ardo calls a recipe for recognising bad men.

## Recipe for recognising bad men

*Tools*:
Eyes of a cat
Ears of an elephant
Smartness of a fox
Awareness of an owl

*Ingredients*:
*gododle*
*jirjiroole*
*qorqode*
*quduuc*
*macangag*
*xile bilaal*
*hinaase*

Like the little animal, which runs round all day digging many burrows and jumping from one burrow to the next, *gododle* is the name for a womaniser.

Like the sun bush, which turns its leaves, wherever the sun goes, *jirjiroole* is the name for a man who changes quickly.

Like the deep digger insect, which gathers everything in its burrow and is skinned by hunger, *qorqode* is the name for a mean man who counts the shopping.

Like the sad and miserable loner bird, *quduuc* is the name for an unfriendly man who avoids conversation and can't stand commitment.

Like the *xabag*, resin that sticks to the bark of the tree, *macangag* is the name for a man who is arrogant, argumentative, ungrateful and hard.

Like a shallow container or a vessel, *xile bilaal* is an empty man who lacks trust, security and is violent.

Like the man nicknamed *xidhxidh*, the rope tier, *hinaasi* is an obsessive man whose first energy of the day battles with numerous ropes securing every opportunity of entry and escape.

The Way I Live
written and illustrated
ⁱ
by
Rosie

# The way I live

## Written and illustrated by Rosie

ⁱ

Rosie's class were doing a project about their own lifestyles called 'The Way I Live'. Rosie wrote and illustrated this little book which encapsulates the lifestyle of the Romany gypsy community from a child's perspective. The full colour version is much more evocative with a black trailer (caravan) when unhappy and a yellow one when travelling in the sunshine.

*Fran Duncan, co-ordinator of the Consortium of*
*Traveller Education Services in Cleveland*

**Here is my new trailer. Its got two bedrooms, a living room and a shower room.**

In my new trailer we have got three couches. We have got a great big shelf and a big round table.

In my new trailer there are 3 bedrooms.

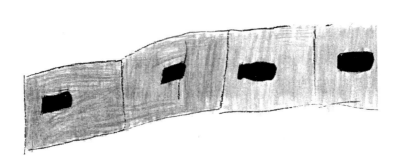

We have got in our trailer a big white kitchen and we have got big bunks.

**This is my shower room.
Its got 1 mirror.**

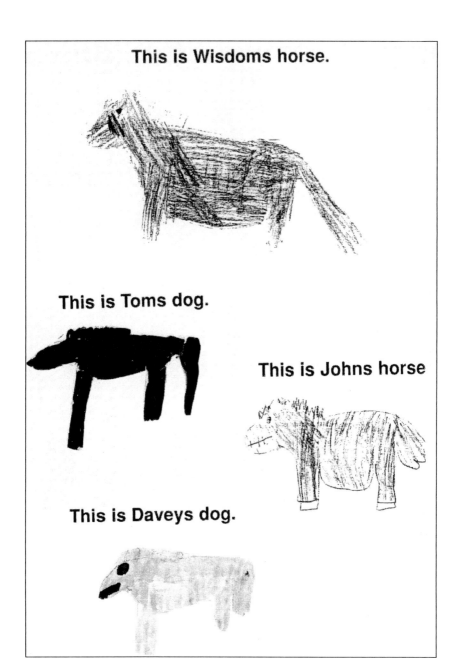

This is Wisdoms horse.

This is Toms dog.

This is Johns horse

This is Daveys dog.

# My best site

**My best site is at Appleby.
There is lots of trailers and lots of
people. I meet my cousins.**

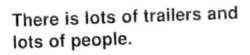

**There is lots of trailers and lots of people.**

Appleby.

**I go up the fair and buy
candy floss and apples.**
**when we come off Appleby
we pull on lay bys and we pull in fields.
Everywhere we pull in the councils come
and they say you'll have to pull off.**

**There is a park across the road.
We move the horses up and about.
We move and you have to park down
because they shift us.**

**one time we said my mams not in, she's
went to the shops and we didn't get the
letter so we didn't pull off.**

# My worst site

My worst site is at Wearton. Its horrible. It's mucky and its boring. The women are always arguing over kids and the warden is always shouting.

My Dad deals with the men and my Mam cleans up. Big boys and little boys throw mud balls.

They complain if you don't sweep your slab.

They're always complaining about something. They complain about dogs. They complain about my Dads horse and its in the field and my Dad argues.

At schools it was horrible. I never had nowt to do - they used to leave you with nothing to do and they never helped you when you needed help.

There was a horrible girl. She was a new starter and she was always fighting and the teacher shouted. I wouldn't do it because it was too hard and I said no to the teacher. I never got a day off only on Saturday and Sunday.

I hated it.

Wearton is horrible and I don't want to go back.

**English Imaginaries
Anglo-British Approaches
to Modernity**
*Kevin Davey*

*Recommended retail price £12.99.
Available to Soundings readers for
£10.99 post free.*

What does it mean to be English in the modern
world? The answer doesn't usually include Nancy Cunard's assault on
Anglo British whitenes, J. B. Priestley's democratic populism, Who
guitarist Pete Townshend's modernist rebellion, Vivienne Westwood's anti-
fashion, David Dabydeen's blackening of the literary and visual canon or
Mark Wallinger's detourement of English oil painting. Kevin Davey,
drawing on the work of Gramsci and Julia Kristeva, argues that it should
and goes on to ask some searching questions about New Labour's vision
of the nation.

> '*With this book the debate about
> Englishness grows up. In his profound
> meditation Kevin Davey puts to shame
> most of the recent spate of essays on this
> fashionable theme.*' Anthony Barnett

# Soundings